Equality and Beyond

George Grier is Coordinator of Anti-Poverty and Social Welfare Programs for the District of Columbia; his wife, Eunice, is Acting Director of the Research Division for the U.S. Commission on Civil Rights. Both studied at the University of Pennsylvania and have acted as consultants to federal, state, and city governments and private agencies on problems of housing, human relations, and urban problems. Together they previously wrote *Privately Developed Interracial Housing*.

Equality and Beyond

◻◼ HOUSING SEGREGATION AND
THE GOALS OF THE GREAT SOCIETY

by George and Eunice Grier

CHICAGO ◼ QUADRANGLE BOOKS ◻ 1966

PREFACE

In 1963 we were asked by the Anti-Defamation League of B'nai B'rith to prepare a revised and updated version of our *Discrimination in Housing: A Handbook of Facts*, first published by the ADL in its Freedom Pamphlet series in 1959. The task proved to be much larger than first anticipated. Not only had earlier statistics on the problem been grossly outdated by the 1960 census, but the outpouring of a huge volume of research and written opinion had greatly expanded the literature. What was required, therefore, was not mere revision but an entirely new work.

As we struggled to comprehend and organize the vast amount of new knowledge, we came to two conclusions. First, while an exhaustive compendium on the problem of housing segregation and discrimination would be useful, such a volume would be somewhat outdated even before it could be published. Second, we were struck both by the

v

magnitude of the problem and by its urgency. Awareness of the impact of growing segregation upon many of the most vital issues of an increasingly urbanized society was made more intense by our concurrent experiences as advisors to various public and private programs aimed at the physical and social renewal and the rational future development of urban areas.

It became increasingly apparent that the Negro ghettos constituted both a major source of many of the problems these programs attempted to solve, and a potent continuing obstacle to their solution. Many such problems would continue to defy rational solution so long as residential segregation remained an overriding factor.

We became convinced that the United States must come to full and frank confrontation with the meaning of racial ghettoization and its concomitant effects; must comprehend the roots of ghettoization in past trends and policies, and the contribution of present policies toward its continuing growth; must recognize that alternatives to these policies do exist; and must decide as a nation whether it wishes to continue along its present course, or to take the steps necessary to remove the ghettos as a prime feature of American life.

Finally, it seemed evident that prompt and decisive action was imperative if this problem was to be solved at all. Failure to take action would, in effect, be a vote in favor of the continued growth of residential segregation with all that this implied; and indecision for much longer might well carry the problem past the point of practical solution.

This line of thinking brought the book to its present form and substance. Because it is meant to stimulate public debate rather than to close it off, it is a short book and one which raises more questions than it answers. Because we hope it will reach a broad spectrum of the informed public and not just a limited group of the technically sophisticated, it is written in non-technical language. For that same reason, its handling of some topics may not completely satisfy technicians. As a treatment of a profoundly complicated problem, it doubtless has many shortcomings; but hopefully the American public itself will write the final and definitive answers.

Many persons and organizations contributed to the information and thinking that went into this book. Some of these sources, but by no means all, are listed in the Notes at the end of the volume; whether listed or not, we are grateful to all. We would be greatly remiss, however, if we failed to grant specific acknowledgment to a few whose assistance has been particularly helpful. Most of the manuscript was prepared while we were principally employed by the Washington Center for Metropolitan Studies. We drew heavily upon work performed for that organization as well as upon the broad exposure to contemporary thinking on urban problems which the Center afforded us.

The American Friends Service Committee (Quakers) deserves thanks for at least two reasons. First, it was instrumental in bringing us into contact with the field of race and housing for the first time a decade ago. Second, its pioneer Housing Opportunities Program has provided us with a continuing and infinitely valuable acquaintance with the realities that confront citizen efforts toward desegregation both locally and nationally.

The National Committee Against Discrimination in Housing has been a lavish and always dependable source of information both on legislative developments and on private citizen action. There is no question that without the devoted work of this organization and of the Quakers there would not only be much less knowledge about the problems we have attempted to outline but much less hope for effective solutions.

To the Anti-Defamation League of B'nai B'rith we owe not only the impetus for this volume but support of many kinds in its preparation. Oscar Cohen, National Program Director, inspired and commissioned it. Stan Wexler, Publications Director, shepherded it through the shoals both of its authors' competing responsibilities and of the editorial process. The incisive pencil of Harris Dienstfrey, engaged by the League to edit the manuscript, substantially im-, proved the form and structure. All displayed virtually limit-less patience during the months when the manuscript was proceeding erratically toward completion.

None of these organizations or individuals, of course, is responsible for specific opinions expressed or for errors of omission or commission. That responsibility, as always, rests solely with the authors.

GEORGE AND EUNICE GRIER

CONTENTS

Equality and Beyond

I. THE TASK AT HAND

The United States today faces an all-out battle against one of its most protracted and fundamental domestic problems. The confrontation is long overdue, and the solution requires efforts that will have to be much more intense and far-reaching than most Americans probably now realize.

The problem is racial segregation and discrimination, and the task before the country is to undo the consequences of its prolonged and systematic repression of the rights of one-tenth of its population. In particular, it must deal decisively with the enforced segregation of these citizens into limited residential areas — geographic separation which carries with it profound social, economic, physical, and psychological effects. Recent large-scale population movements have complicated this task enormously, creating many new obstacles in the way of its solution. Worse, the population shifts now have gained a momentum which tends to be self-sustaining.

The United States has already paid a heavy price for the practice of racial segregation and discrimination and their concomitant effects. That cost is almost certainly very little compared to what lies ahead in the remaining years of this century if the nation does not take vigorous steps to eliminate the racial ghetto, a social evil about which it can no longer afford to be complacent.

It should be said, of course, that during the past several years, the struggle to eliminate segregation and discrimination in various areas of life has seen a number of noteworthy gains. These perhaps have been overshadowed by highly publicized episodes of racial violence and a growing number of racial protests. However, in a certain sense, even incidents of this sort represent a change for the better. They can arise only in a situation where rigid repression has somewhat abated. Progress certainly has been neither quick nor easy, nor has it been without considerable pain. But for all of this, it is still occurring within the basic American framework of representative government, free speech, and the democratic tradition of voluntary association.

A few brief comparisons with the recent past will indicate the nature and the degree of this progress. In the field of employment, the situation has changed significantly from the early years of World War II—when many munitions manufacturers refused to hire non-white workers despite stringent labor shortages, and when a Philadelphia shipbuilding firm went so far as to operate two shipyards, one staffed by whites and the other by Negroes. Now, even in the deep South, more and more defense contractors are hiring and promoting across racial lines. The recently enacted Civil Rights Act can greatly accelerate progress toward equality of opportunity in employment throughout the nation.

Again, in the area of public facilities, the Civil Rights Act assures free access by Negroes to theaters, restaurants, hotels, and stores. Vestiges of resistance are fast disappearing. Throughout much of the North and West, these rights have for some years now been protected by state or local laws. Few such laws existed as little as two decades ago, and almost anywhere in the nation Negro citizens constantly faced the humiliating possibility of being denied entrance to public places because of their race; when this occurred, they had no legal recourse.

In the field of housing, it is a great distance indeed from the immediate postwar period, when governmental agencies enforced racial segregation in federally aided housing, to the present day, when governmental policy is dominated by the order signed by President Kennedy late in 1962 prohibiting discrimination in all housing receiving federal assistance.

Though progress often seems painfully slow, especially to those who bear the burden of discrimination, it is nonetheless true that in less than a generation America has moved forward from an almost complete lack of public concern for the civil rights of its racial minorities to a situation in which, under the pressure of public opinion, the country increasingly guards these rights by law.

At the heart of the progress now taking place is the recognition by a growing number of Negro and white citizens of the serious dangers that widespread social inequities and racial separation pose to the stability and continued progress of the nation as a whole. Large population changes, which began decades ago but accelerated enormously just after World War II, have made increasingly clear the integral relationship between race and a large variety of critical national problems—in the areas of urban renewal, employment, poverty, and education. As a result, the problem of race has been pushed to the forefront of the national consciousness.

The national concern stems, in large part, from the fact that population changes have now enlarged the Negro "ghettos" of many major urban areas to the point where they

5

increasingly dominate the cities of which they are a part. But America has yet to come to grips with the central phenomenon of these ghettos themselves—and the fact that their continuing existence and enlargement perils the gains of the recent past and the prospects for the future. This book addresses itself to the problem of growing racial segregation in housing in the face of a national commitment to desegregation and equal opportunity — to the causes, the effects, and above all to the urgent need for effective action.

The most comprehensive and best-enforced laws designed to protect the equal rights of citizens in schools, public facilities, and even employment can only be partly successful so long as geographic barriers continue to impede many of those affected from taking full advantage of their newly guaranteed rights. Equality under the law is not enough so long as residential segregation sets differential frameworks under which that equality can be claimed by the two racial groups concerned. And the current victories against discrimination may prove hollow indeed if the next several decades see racial patterns in housing continue to develop along lines which create two separate Americas, one black and one white.

POPULATION CHANGES AND THE PROBLEM OF RACE

During the decade between 1950 and 1960, each of the nation's fifteen largest metropolitan areas registered larger increases in Negro than white populations.[1] In every case, moreover, the preponderant portion of the Negro increase was within the area's central city. At the same time, most of these cities also lost a sizable portion of their white population. In every *major American city* the result was a dramatic increase in both the numbers and the proportion of its people who were Negro.

6

A few statistics will indicate the general magnitude of the change. In the city of New York the Negro population increased by 46 percent; in Chicago, by 65 percent; in Philadelphia, by 41 percent; in Washington, D.C., by 47 percent; in Los Angeles, by 96 percent; in Milwaukee, by 187 percent. Striking increases also occurred in many smaller metropolitan areas. In Syracuse, Rochester, New Haven, San Diego, and Fort Wayne, for example, the Negro populations approximately doubled.

By 1960 Negroes constituted over half the population of Washington, D.C.; over one-third of the populations of Baltimore and New Orleans; over one-fourth of the populations of Philadelphia, Detroit, Cleveland, and St. Louis; and over one-fifth of those of Chicago and Houston. Today, Negroes in a growing number of cities constitute significantly more than the approximate 10 percent of the population they comprise across the nation as a whole.

In almost all the areas, Negroes are concentrated in the heart of the central city. This pattern of residence is most dramatically illustrated by the statistics describing Washington, D.C., the first major American city to contain a Negro majority. Negroes make up one-fourth of Washington's entire *metropolitan* population, including both city and suburbs. This proportion has remained virtually constant since 1920. In the *city* of Washington, however, the Negro population rose sharply during the same time span from approximately one-fourth to well over half. And in the *suburbs* it declined from about one-fourth to only 6 percent.

By 1980, at the latest, several other cities are likely to join Washington in having populations that are over 50 percent Negro. Baltimore, Cleveland, Detroit, New Orleans, Philadelphia, and St. Louis all are leading candidates. Indeed, Baltimore and New Orleans may pass the 50 percent mark before 1970.

Thus Negroes are rapidly becoming the dominant population group in the centers of America's industrial and com-

7

mercial wealth. When most Negroes lived in the rural areas of a generally impoverished South, it was possible to think of discrimination as a parochial problem and so more or less disregard it. But this attitude is no longer possible. Now the lower incomes of Negroes, their frequently deprived educational and cultural backgrounds, the greater concentration of social problems and health difficulties in the Negro community—all these press with increasing force upon central cities throughout the country. And as the numbers of Negroes increase, so their areas of residence expand.[2]

To undo the effects of segregation, it would perhaps have been sufficient at one time merely to create conditions under which Negroes were no longer denied full opportunity in any area, and then to let matters take their course. Most Negroes would have found a productive place in the nation's economic and social structure in no more time than it took the various groups of white immigrants who arrived on American shores with many of the educational and financial deficiencies that characterized the slaves brought in bondage from Africa. But, under present conditions, mere nondiscrimination is no longer enough. Today the United States confronts the much larger task of *reversing* the cumulative effects of generation upon generation of enforced disadvantage. It must do this, moreover, in a context in which the two large racial groups upon whose cooperation success ultimately depends have more and more become two isolated geographic units.

The problems are further complicated by the characteristics of many of the whites who remain in the cities. Between 1950 and 1960, nearly two-thirds of the nation's *total* population increase—an increase that was overwhelmingly white—took place in the *suburbs* of its major metropolitan areas. During that time whites left the cities in large numbers, and those who left were primarily the younger and more upwardly mobile families. Those who remained behind were, in large part, the old, the poor, the single, the sick and disabled, and the socially disadvantaged—in general, the people who share with Negroes (though for different reasons) many of the same social and economic deprivations. For the most part, these are not the raw materials for a vigorous and economically solvent urban leadership. Perhaps more important in the long run, they do not constitute the kind of population which can be expected to maintain or increase its numbers.

SEGREGATION AND THE DILEMMAS OF URBAN AMERICA

America has lived with discrimination and segregation for so long that by now effects have become causes. And the interrelationships of cause and effect have become increasingly entangled with each other and with ever wider areas of concern that now touch all aspects of the country's urban life.

A relatively simple example of these complexities can be seen in the recent conflicts concerning the consequences of "de facto" segregation in Northern public schools. While these schools are (for the most part) desegregated in principle, because of the surrounding residential patterns they very often are segregated in practice.[3]

Such "de facto" segregation tends to create poor, inadequately serviced schools. The concentration of culturally deprived Negro children makes it difficult to provide the intensive programs they need to reach an equal footing with their white contemporaries. The problem is exacerbated by the fact that the schools usually are located in the older and more depressed neighborhoods of the city. Both the schools and their surroundings are often in physical and social decay. Thus, in addition to everything else, it becomes difficult to attract or keep good teachers.

Negro groups, with some white help, have fought to eliminate such conditions. One solution has been to bus

9

Negro children to better schools which are under-utilized and for the most part are predominantly white. This approach has met with strenuous resistance from many parents (most of them white, but sometimes including Negroes of more secure economic position) who live in the better neighborhoods and whose children attend the schools there. Some observers fear that to pursue a bus transport program against the protest of such parents would cause many of them to remove their children from the school in question; or, more drastically, to move their entire family out of the city itself, thus tending to re-create the conditions the program sought to overcome.

Another alternative is to upgrade the Negro schools where they now stand, i.e., within their segregated neighborhoods. What are the problems here? Even to refurbish the buildings and put them in satisfactory condition would be extremely expensive. Moreover, the ability of the schools to provide the necessary educational improvements would be severely limited by the general strain which has been placed upon the taxing powers of municipal governments by the white migration to the suburbs. Yet a further complication is created by the fact that a systematic effort to overcome accumulated disadvantage requires programs and facilities superior to those enjoyed by most middle-class white students. In addition, some civil rights groups have opposed rebuilding of ghetto schools on the ground that this would serve to reinforce "de facto" segregation.

Similar difficulties surround many attempts at urban renewal.[4] Because Negroes tend to be concentrated in the decaying central districts, they often are the ones displaced from their homes under renewal programs. Some civil rights groups have gone so far as to call urban renewal "Negro removal." And in a certain sense, regardless of the motivations involved, this is what many renewal programs inevitably must be, given the geographic coincidence of Negroes and poor housing.

The relocation of Negro families creates another sort of

problem. Many relocated families are moved into better, essentially white or interracial neighborhoods nearby. The white residents frequently panic and move away; and so too do the economically higher-status Negro residents who may be in the area. The result, in many cases, has been to lower the quality of neighborhoods close to renewal sites, and on occasion to create another area suitable for renewal.

Renewal programs tend to bring to light many of the most depressing and difficult social problems faced by today's city. The problems have been there for some time. Renewal does not create them, although, depending upon the skill and human sensitivity with which it is conducted, it can ameliorate or worsen them. It is quite understandable why renewal has so frequently become the focal point of community conflicts that contain a strong element of racial tension. It is understandable too why some observers now believe that renewal cannot succeed within the present framework of a racially segregated urban environment.

Many other problems of the cities today are exacerbated by racial segregation. The Negro ghettos have long bred crime, violence, disease, and cumulative disadvantage. As the ghettos grow larger, these problems also grow greater and more intractable, in part because of their geographic concentration. City governments have struggled painfully, but few successfully, with the difficulty of financing the many kinds of facilities and services necessary to cope with these worsening physical and social problems. One potent contributor to this dilemma has been the fact that the suburban expansion has taken from the city many of its more affluent citizens.[5]

The tendency of those who have bettered themselves financially to move outward from the urban centers is hardly a new one. Throughout American history there has been a steady centrifugal movement of more fortunate families in search of more room, better homes, and freedom from the hazards and annoyances of congested central areas. Until recent decades, however, this movement took few of them beyond the city lines. Today, almost all move beyond into the politically separate suburbs; and their numbers include not only the wealthy but also the much more numerous middle class.

The cities, left to fend for themselves with a population which in the aggregate becomes relatively less affluent and more and more heavily Negro, have turned to the federal government for aid. Solutions to their problems are now being sought through massive new federal legislation in such fields as housing, education, and poverty. The new programs are necessary but expensive; and unquestionably the billions already appropriated are only the beginning.

If race creates perplexing obstacles in the efforts to halt the physical and social decay of urban neighborhoods, it likewise complicates the task of planning effectively for suburban expansion. The recent rapid growth of the nation's metropolitan complexes makes it essential that future population increases proceed in a less geographically haphazard fashion. During the 1950's, choice land on the periphery of the larger cities was gobbled up at a ferocious rate. In metropolitan Philadelphia, for example, while the population of the "urbanized" or heavily built-up portion of the area increased by only 24 percent, the geographic size of this portion nearly doubled.[6]

This reckless consumption of land cannot continue for much longer. Commuting distances are already excessive, and in many places nearby metropolitan areas are rapidly running together. Philadelphia has already joined with Trenton, New Jersey, and Wilmington, Delaware, in one continuous urban mass. Baltimore and Washington, once forty miles apart, have eaten up almost all the space between them. Los Angeles has run together with Long Beach; New York City with several important cities in New Jersey and Connecticut; Detroit with Ann Arbor.[7]

Municipalities are grappling in various ways with the challenging task of making more efficient use of the land which still remains within feasible traveling distance. The aim of these plans is to keep the metropolitan areas fit places to live, with a reasonable balance of the various elements—homes, commercial and cultural centers, adequate transit facilities, industries, parks, and so forth—that together constitute a human environment. Once again, the problems of race come to the forefront.

In metropolitan Washington, D.C., for example, regional planning agencies recently devised a "Plan for the Year 2000,"[8] setting forth general principles to meet the needs of a population expected to grow to more than twice its present size before the end of the century. The plan suggested that future growth be channeled along six radial "corridors" extending outward in star fashion from the central city. Highways and transit lines would run along the corridors with centers of commerce and other service areas spaced at appropriate intervals. To preserve as much as possible of the green countryside, parks and open recreational areas would be placed between the corridors.

The plan, however, failed to take into account one vital consideration: the effect of race. If the movement of the city's population continues in its present direction, three corridors will be heavily Negro. They will have their central origins in neighborhoods which currently are Negro and which already are expanding outward in the directions proposed by the plan. The other three corridors will be primarily white, and in similar fashion will originate in the only white residential areas that remain within the city of Washington. Thus segregation will be extended for an indefinite period into the new suburbs, and in a way that almost certainly will help to perpetuate the current relative status of whites and Negroes.[9]

It is also possible, of course, that restrictive real estate practices will choke off Negro population expansion along the three suburban corridors most likely to accommodate it. If this should occur, Negroes will be forced back into the city of Washington, quickly overwhelming those areas which still remain white or interracial and making the District's population virtually all Negro within a short time.

13

THE HEART OF THE MATTER

At the root of most such dilemmas is residential segregation. If Negroes were more evenly dispersed throughout the metropolitan areas, not only would the concentration of urban problems be reduced but the resources available to deal with them would be immensely increased. And the tendency of those problems that center on race to extend themselves geographically and to perpetuate themselves in time would be sharply curtailed if not entirely eliminated.

For several years, legal prohibitions against racial discrimination in housing have received much publicity. These prohibitions, however, are neither exhaustive nor perfect. Enforcement procedures also have often been slow, cumbersome, and uneven. But even if the laws and their enforcement were complete and perfect in all aspects, they would not be sufficient to do the job that now exists.

The magnitude of the task is suggested by the statistics that George Schermer has computed for the Philadelphia metropolitan area.[10] Schermer has estimated that just to prevent current Negro neighborhoods from expanding any further would necessitate the annual movement from these neighborhoods of 6,000 Negro households. Moreover, to disperse the Negro population evenly throughout the Philadelphia metropolis by the year 2000 would necessitate the entry of 9,700 Negro households into currently white districts and the entry of 3,700 white families into currently Negro areas—*each year from 1961 through 2000.*

As things now stand, the year 2000 will probably see Negro majorities in the core cities of most of the nation's major metropolitan areas, with a number of these cities being almost entirely Negro. The overriding fact is that most Negroes are simply too poor to afford private housing at the prices which now prevail in many of the newer suburbs. In 1959, the latest date for which complete statistics are available, approximately one-fourth of the Negro families in the North had incomes of $6,000 or more. Recently there has been a slow trickle of more affluent Negro families into predominantly white suburbs, and an increasing trickle of whites into more or less Negro neighborhoods —usually rehabilitated under private auspices—within the city.[11] But neither movement touches the key problem: the low income of much of the Negro market.

The dilemmas posed to the United States by residential segregation are put in sharper focus by the current war against poverty. Can poverty among Negroes ever be eliminated in the face of their increasingly rigid segregation within the metropolitan centers? On the other hand, can metropolitan areas be desegregated as long as the majority of Negroes remain poor? As segregation continues to grow, and Negroes reach numerical predominance in more and more urban centers, will the central cities which house the bulk of the nation's industrial and commercial life find themselves less and less able to cope with their problems, despite massive federal aid? What then will be the answer for the metropolitan complexes where two-thirds of America's population currently reside, and where as much as 85 percent of the nation may live by the year 2000?

The task of overcoming and reversing the accumulated racial inequities of generations, and of eliminating the growing racial separation which accompanies and helps perpetuate them, is not yet hopeless. But each year in which effective action is delayed, the task becomes less and less manageable. To eliminate segregation now calls for national resolve and a sustained effort of many years. It will entail a varied yet coordinated set of basically national programs that must all be carried forward within the framework of the democratic ethos.

Do the American people possess the will and the courage to go *beyond* nondiscrimination and to move into a realm of positive programs for undoing the harm that segregation has already brought the country? And if they do not, are they prepared to accept the profoundly deleterious consequences that are bound to fall upon American society?

15

II. THE SPREAD
OF SEGREGATION

The huge urban Negro populations of the 1960's—exceeding a quarter-million persons in ten of the nation's fifteen largest metropolitan areas, and topping a half-million in four of them—constitute relatively new phenomena on the American scene. An auto tour through New York's Harlem and Bedford-Stuyvesant areas, or Chicago's South Side, or through North Central Philadelphia, or through almost any section of Washington, D.C., will prove to even the least perceptive of observers the extent to which Negro residential districts today dominate the cores of our cities.[1]

In addition, for the first time in American history, substantial Negro "ghettos" have emerged in many medium-sized cities, which previously could regard such physical sores with some condescension as the exclusive problem of a few urban giants.[2]

Not all the predominantly Negro areas of today's cities are slums, however, and this too is a comparatively recent development. The movement of white families to the suburbs has opened up a number of highly desirable living places for a minority of Negro families that now can afford them. Thus some of the finest residential sections in cities like Washington and Philadelphia — sections which once were predominantly white — have become all, or heavily, Negro. The physical character and general flavor of such neighborhoods have changed little. Imposing stone and brick homes still stand on skillfully landscaped and immaculately maintained lawns. Only the color of the residents has changed.

Yet these too are *Negro* neighborhoods, and—like the sprawling all-white subdivisions surrounding the cities, or like the less desirable central districts where most Negroes are obliged to live—they betoken the growth of patterns of residential segregation which are splitting our metropolitan areas into two huge enclaves, each the territory of a single race. Segregation itself is not new, but never before has it manifested itself on such a giant and destructive scale.[3]

HOW IT GREW

The current pattern and scale of racial segregation is the product of several forces—some of which have had little or nothing to do with race, and some of which have been the results of public policy decisions directed toward quite different ends. Certainly America as a nation cannot escape responsibility for its past misdeeds. But the search for solutions to the present situation cannot proceed realistically if it is not realized that forces both broader than and different from racial discrimination have helped produce it.

The Burgeoning Metropolitan Complexes. One of the largest contributors to the spread of segregated patterns has been the rapid *overall* expansion of America's metropolitan areas.[4]

This expansion is the combined product of national

17

population growth and increasing urbanization. As the country has grown more populous, its inhabitants increasingly have chosen to make large metropolitan complexes their centers of work and residence. A century ago Americans numbered only 31 million, and about one-fifth of them, some 6 million, lived in urban areas. By 1920 the total population had increased to 105 million, and the number in urban areas had risen to 54 million, or roughly one-half. Today the total population nears 200 million, and the urban proportion stands at over 125 million, or roughly two-thirds.

The decline of agriculture as a source of employment has contributed to the growth of the metropolitan areas. Over the past two census decades, farm residents have moved to cities at such a rate that their number has declined by several millions at the same time that the national population has expanded at an unprecedented pace.

Population growth in general has accelerated sharply in the years following World War II. The largest ten-year population increase in the nation's history took place between 1950 and 1960, an increase of twenty-eight millions. About 85 percent of the increase was contained within the 212 metropolitan areas, many of which grew to half again their size, or even more.

One result of these increases has been the emergence of "super cities" that overflow old municipal boundaries. During the 1950's the population surrounding America's major cities grew in the aggregate by almost 50 percent, and in many specific locations by far more than that. Between 1950 and 1960 the suburbs of New York City increased in population by 75 percent; those of Chicago by 70 percent; of Detroit by 79 percent; and of San Francisco and Oakland combined by 55 percent.

It is this general pattern of growth—in itself a neutral development as far as race is concerned—that has provided the setting for the two concurrent and related trends that have greatly increased the spread of segregation: the movement of whites to the suburbs and their replacement in the central cities by Negroes.

The Exclusive Suburbs. At the end of World War II there was a great and pressing shortage of housing, the result of a backlog of need accumulated through a decade and a half of economic depression and world conflict. The American nation set out on a massive effort to satisfy that need.

It naturally turned to the suburbs to do so, since most central cities had little remaining land suitable for development. What was not equally natural, however, was that the residents of the resulting communities were almost exclusively white. This development was the product of several interrelated public and private decisions.

One of the most central was the public decision to deal with the housing shortage chiefly through the private enterprise system. Such government mechanisms as were mobilized to aid in the task, especially the mortgage-guaranteeing provisions of the Federal Housing Administration and the Veterans Administration, were all directed to encourage the efforts of private enterprise.[5]

In physical terms, the home-building industry did its job extremely well. Indeed, the result can be counted as one of the major achievements of a nation that has never been satisfied with small accomplishments. Almost every year from the end of World War II through 1960, more than one million new dwelling units were constructed and occupied, a figure which was twice the rate at which new families were formed. As a consequence, despite the high concurrent rate of population growth, the 1960 census showed Americans to be far better housed than ever before. General overcrowding and "doubling up" (two or more families in one dwelling) had been sharply reduced. So had the number of dilapidated and otherwise substandard housing units. The entire population benefited to some degree from these improvements—even Negroes, although, as always, they remained less adequately housed than whites.[6]

But the decision to let private enterprise satisfy the

housing shortage carried with it certain important implications that significantly affected the country's patterns of residence. For one thing, it meant that housing as a general rule was built only for those groups that could afford to pay a price that would allow the contractor a reasonable margin of profit. Rarely were the houses offered for rent. Further, the new housing, supported as it was by the federal loan-guarantee programs, was aimed almost exclusively at the market of young, expanding families. Federal mortgage underwriting provisions were adjusted to grant the most lenient terms possible (including low down-payments and extended repayment periods) to the family just getting started in life and willing to commit itself to the responsibilities of a mortgage. Groups or individuals who did not fit this category — smaller families, older people, single persons, people with low incomes, individuals who sought dwellings for rent rather than for sale—all were required to satisfy their needs chiefly through the older housing left vacant by the people who had moved to new homes in the suburbs. The older housing was located, of course, chiefly within the central cities.

It may be that a good number of young white families would have preferred to remain in the cities, close to work and to older relatives. But the government did not allow a family with good future prospects but momentarily limited income equally good terms on the mortgages of older homes in the cities. The suburbs were their only practical alternative.

Very little publicly subsidized low-rent housing was produced during this period, and hardly any of it in the suburbs. From 1950 to 1960 the increase amounted to only about 300,000 dwelling units out of a total increase of more than twelve million homes—that is, only 2½ percent—and most of the units were constructed within the central cities. By a general if implicit consensus among members of the real estate and home-building industries, federal and local governments, and, in most cases, those people already in residence, low-income families, regardless of race or origin, were kept out of the new suburbs.[7]

Most Negro families would have been economically incapable of purchasing a new home there in any case. Generations of discrimination in employment and education had seen to that. A market analysis by the University of Pennsylvania's Institute for Urban Studies, undertaken at the peak of the postwar housing boom in the mid-1950's, revealed that only about half of one percent of homes priced at over $12,000 in Philadelphia had then been purchased by Negro families, and ascribed this fact chiefly to economic limitations.[8] These figures may be taken as more or less typical.

But even if Negro families had had the resources to buy, they seldom were allowed to do so. A variety of estimates during the middle and late fifties agreed that for the nation as a whole, and in a number of individual metropolitan areas, less than 2 percent of all new homes produced with FHA insurance had been made available to Negroes.[9] These percentages were mostly the result of discriminatory practices on the part of individual builders and financing firms. But even where such practices were not being followed, the federal government itself often required exclusion of Negroes as a condition of its participation.[10]

Underpinning many of these practices was the widespread public belief that neighborhoods were better off if the people within them all belonged to the same general socio-economic groupings and had the same ethnic or racial origins. In practice, of course, this commitment to neighborhood homogeneity operated chiefly to exclude individuals who fell *below* a certain status level, not those who were above it. The latter, however, usually "excluded" themselves in neighborhoods that were of their own level of status. The result, in general, was that vertical differences in social standing spread out horizontally across the face of an urbanizing America.

Attempts to maintain neighborhood exclusiveness—particularly on the part of upper-status groups—by no means originated in the postwar years. For many decades, a barrage of methods had been employed to separate residentially the different groups that together had devised the ethical precepts and built the material prosperity of the world's most powerful democracy. Real estate zoning codes and certain marketing practices set prices so high as to exclude many members of minority groups from "better" neighborhoods. But price alone was not sufficient to keep all minority members out, so other devices were added. One quite frankly discriminatory device, the racial zoning ordinance, was outlawed by the Supreme Court in 1917. In its place, builders expanded restrictive covenants which prohibited the keeping of chickens and goats to prohibit the residence of Jews, Orientals, Negroes, and other groups as well. In 1948 the Supreme Court ruled that covenants by race and religion were legally unenforceable in the courts (but did not outlaw their voluntary use).[11]

The standards for acceptance into or exclusion from a neighborhood were based on the most crass and superficial of criteria which in some instances exposed their practitioners to well-deserved ridicule—as with the "point system" that earned the Detroit suburb of Grosse Pointe a national reputation for snobbery and stuffiness—or brought them public censure, as with the restrictive covenant against Jews of the W. C. and A. N. Miller Company, developers of the exclusive Spring Valley section of Washington, D.C.[12] In the latter case, noted public figures like Secretary of State Dean Rusk publicly announced their refusal to sign the covenant, and as a result of community indignation the firm recently was forced to withdraw from a valuable urban renewal contract.

General public opinion on the virtues of neighborhood homogeneity changed somewhat following the Supreme Court decision of 1948. Jews in particular began to find it easier to obtain access to neighborhoods on the basis of pocketbook and preference. Toward the end of the 1950's even Negroes began to find a few breaks in the traditional barriers, though, as always, the benefits came later for them than for others.

Yet, paradoxically, the postwar era also saw one particular form of neighborhood exclusiveness extended in practice on a scale never before imagined. The chief cause was the working practices of suburban developers, who built tracts containing hundreds and even thousands of homes all in one narrow price range. The prices of different subdivisions varied considerably, but within any single one the range was comparatively small. Americans of many faiths and backgrounds thus found themselves living beside people with whom they often shared little except a similar money income. The one group still excluded—a group for whom economic criteria were not considered an adequate basis for entry—was Negroes.[13]

The Emergence of the "Negro" Cities. In recent years there have been large-scale population movements both from the center of the United States toward its boundaries (especially to the seacoasts and to the Great Lakes region) and from the South to the North. This general migration, most expert sources agree, has been both "pulled" and "pushed." It has been "pulled" by the job opportunities and other attractions of the major cities, especially of those located on the fringes of the nation. It has been "pushed" by the shrinking labor needs in agriculture, particularly in the depressed portions of the rural South. Both Negroes and whites took part in this movement, but the effect on Negro patterns of residence was particularly striking. In 1950 the states with the largest Negro populations were all in the South and the Southwest: Georgia, North Carolina, Mississippi, Alabama, and Texas. Today, the state with the largest Negro population is New York.[14]

Most of the migrants, both whites and Negroes, have been the poorly skilled. But in most cases the whites have been absorbed into the society and economy of the urban-industrial complexes much more readily. Within only a few

23

years, many were prepared to move to the new suburbs. The Negroes, on the other hand, have ended up as semi-permanent inhabitants of central city slums.

Though the Negro component of the migration was large, it was not as large as popular opinion would have it, either proportionately or in terms of absolute numbers. As an extreme example, in metropolitan Washington during the 1950's, whites coming to the national capital area in search of jobs and homes outnumbered Negroes almost three to one. (Over the decade, incoming nonwhites averaged fewer than sixteen persons per day.)[15]

Nor, again despite popular opinion, has the fertility of urban Negroes been much greater than that of whites. During the postwar years *both* groups bore children in America's metropolitan areas at a rate that fully merits the "explosive" terminology we often reserve for less developed nations. The white increase occurred in the suburbs, however; the Negro increase took place in the central cities. A comparative analysis of fertility ratios in metropolitan Washington revealed that whites in several of the newer suburbs had substantially *higher* levels of fertility than did Negroes in the city of Washington.

But the combination of all these factors — rapid urbanization, the concentration of Negro population growth within the cities, the migration of young and fertile white families to the suburbs, the fact that subsequent childbearing among the two racial groups has both reinforced and perpetuated trends begun by selective migration and segregation — these interacting forces have produced the same general effects in metropolitan areas throughout the country: central cities that are increasingly Negro, suburbs that are almost exclusively white.

The Negro increase within the cities, and its concentration in highly restricted districts, has often been listed as a major reason for the white migration to the suburbs. Advocates of this position have also maintained that antipathy toward incoming Negroes often forced whites out of the cities faster than Negroes could fill the gap. (A sizable minority of the central cities in the nation's 212 metropolitan areas actually lost population from 1950 to 1960.)

But a close look at several cities puts this easy and apparently reasonable conclusion in doubt. For example, one of the largest percentage declines in total population during the 1950's occurred in Binghamton, New York, which lost about 6 percent of its population, or nearly 5,000 of its 80,000 inhabitants. However, Binghamton is one of the few cities in New York which has *not* experienced a significant influx of Negroes. Its Negro population, numbering less than 1,200 in 1960, has grown by only a few hundred persons in the past twenty years.

The situation in Syracuse, a nearby city, has been something of the reverse. While its Negro population approximately doubled during the 1950's, rising from about 5,000 to over 11,000, the total population declined by only 2 percent, or about 5,000 persons out of over 200,000. Even more striking is the case of Niagara Falls, where the Negro population again approximately doubled, increasing by about 3,000, and the total population rose as well, by about 12 percent, or 11,000 people.

Similar anomalies can be found in a number of other cities. San Diego, for example, was among the nation's leaders both in *total* increase (about 70 percent) and *Negro* increase (about double for the decade). The city's suburbs also grew more rapidly than those of almost any other of the nation's major metropolitan areas. One of the few areas which exceeded it was Minneapolis-St. Paul, where the Negro influx has been relatively slight.

Clearly, factors other than racial antipathy have been behind the growth of the suburbs and the depletion and transformation of the cities. It may even be that Negro population increase prevented a more complete desertion of the decaying core areas than would naturally have occurred as an increasingly prosperous white population sought better housing than these areas could provide.

25

THE CASE OF WASHINGTON

The three adjoining maps show the combined effect of the forces we have been discussing upon the racial patterns of one city, Washington, D.C. The maps show the city's composition by skin color according to the census tracts* for 1940, 1950, and 1960.[16] (In what follows, the terms "nonwhite" and "Negro" will be used interchangeably. In metropolitan Washington, less than 1 percent of the nonwhite population is other than Negro.)

In 1940 Washington had three relatively small areas of heavy Negro concentration, represented by the black areas on the map. Surrounding each were larger neighborhoods of substantial but lower Negro proportion. The bulk of the city's total land area contained only a small percentage of Negroes.

In 1950 the geographic pattern was much the same. Even though there had been an increase of almost 100,000 Negroes during the decade, they were still living in much the same areas in which they had been concentrated ten years earlier, with only a slight expansion outward. As a result, there was a considerable rise in overcrowding and doubling-up of Negro families.

During the 1950's the dam broke. The map for 1960 shows a vast increase in the size of the areas in which Negroes constituted at least 75 percent of the population. There has also been a substantial growth in the number of neighborhoods where Negroes resided in smaller but still appreciable proportions. In short, the existing Negro ghetto had both expanded and consolidated, and at the same time

*Census tracts are small areas into which cities and their surrounding suburbs are divided for census purposes. The criteria used in defining a tract are complex, but generally they represent an effort to demarcate areas of relatively homogeneous composition. Once selected, however, tract boundaries usually remain unchanged from one census to the next, although large and sparsely settled tracts may sometimes be subdivided as their populations grow.

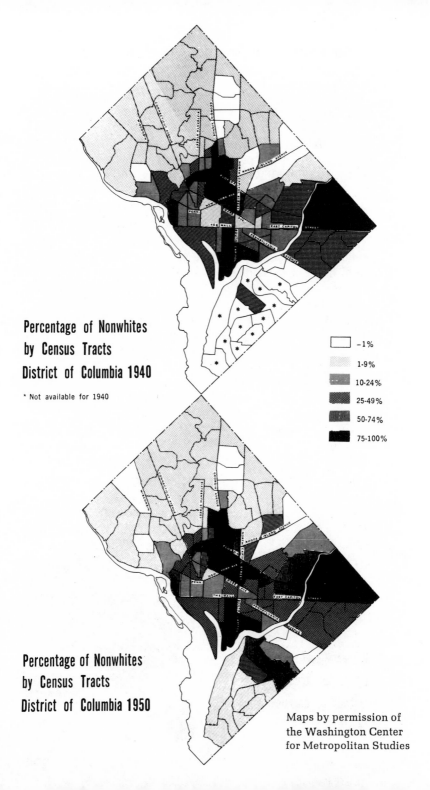

Percentage of Nonwhites
by Census Tracts
District of Columbia 1940

* Not available for 1940

-1%

1-9%

10-24%

25-49%

50-74%

75-100%

Percentage of Nonwhites
by Census Tracts
District of Columbia 1950

Maps by permission of
the Washington Center
for Metropolitan Studies

Negroes had entered many areas previously closed to them.

One immediate positive result of these changes was a reduction in overcrowding and doubling-up. But a more critical negative consequence was an increase in the extent of segregation. The number of census tracts where non-whites made up 75 percent or more of the population approximately doubled during the 1950's, and the number of tracts where whites constituted 90 percent or more of the total declined by almost the same factor. Moreover, the number of tracts where Negroes had constituted 25 to 74 percent of the total population — where, at least in gross statistical terms, some degree of residential desegregation could have been said to exist—also declined.

These maps also reveal that, during the twenty-year period they cover, large parts of Washington underwent racial change while others did not—an observation that is deceptively simple. A large natural area, Rock Creek Park, cuts the city almost in two, beginning somewhat to the north and west of the geographic center and proceeding

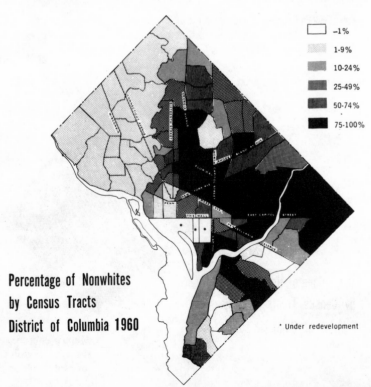

−1%
1-9%
10-24%
25-49%
50-74%
75-100%

**Percentage of Nonwhites
by Census Tracts
District of Columbia 1960**

* Under redevelopment

irregularly northward to the suburbs. In the 1950's Rock Creek Park became the effective barrier to Negro expansion, whose wandering course is clearly visible in the map for 1960. West of the Park there was little racial change; east of it change was extensive. It is common knowledge in Washington that the local real estate industry had decided, whether tacitly or formally, that the neighborhoods east of the park would be freely open to Negro expansion, whereas those on the west would remain reserved for whites. A few Negroes broke across the barrier, but in the main the line held.

A small area in the southeast sector of the city also held firm though change was occurring all around it. Economics alone does not explain the inability of Negroes to obtain homes in this area, since many of its homes were priced lower than in other parts of the city where Negroes had already moved in large numbers.

The internationally famous Georgetown section (marked on the 1960 map by a circle), home of many of the capital city's elite, showed a decline in its Negro population during the 1950's. This decline had begun in the decade before. Once a predominantly Negro neighborhood, Georgetown is an example of racial change in reverse—dramatic disproof of the popular belief that once an area is entered by Negroes it will inevitably become all Negro. Negroes in Georgetown have been steadily displaced by whites; in a short time, if the trend continues, the area will contain practically no Negroes at all.

By any test of mathematics or reason, population changes like these could not be the products of pure chance. While their existence does not conclusively prove the operation of discriminatory practices, it nonetheless suggests that powerful measures have been employed to control the large-scale population shifts which occurred during the fifties. In one tract the Negro population increased from only six persons in 1950 to 4,134 in 1960—or an increase of 69,000 percent![17]

Other major cities show the same general kind of expansion in their patterns of segregation. An analysis by the Philadelphia Commission on Human Relations states that in Philadelphia the number of census tracts with a nonwhite population of 80 percent or more nearly tripled during the fifties.[18] A similar study in New York City, by the municipal Commission on Intergroup Relations, indicated that the total proportion of nonwhites residing in tracts which were 75 percent or more nonwhite increased from 44 percent to 53 percent in the same decade.[19]

Both cities also showed a slight increase in the number of tracts which contained small percentages of nonwhites. This fact reflects the slight lowering of racial bars for Negro families of higher incomes, which occurred largely toward the end of the decade.

In comparison with the greatly increased degree of Negro concentration during the same interval, however, such dispersion has the effect of emptying the sea with an eye dropper. In all, the end of the 1950's saw patterns of residential segregation much more widespread and solidified than they had been at the start.

III. THE COSTS
OF SEGREGATION

Until recent years, arguments for eliminating residential segregation rested almost entirely upon considerations of the injustices inflicted upon the minority. But the majority public, whose active or passive support of discriminatory practices was essential to their continuance, was not especially receptive to such arguments—requiring, as they did, a certain acceptance of moral responsibility coupled with no clear opportunity for personal gain. Similarly, the larger implications of discrimination and segregation for America's democratic ideals and for its world position had little apparent effect in stirring public concern. Segregation persisted and grew.

Current shifts in public attitudes toward the issue are due at least in part to the realization that segregation, in its extended state, now presents clear costs and dangers to the entire nation. Certainly not all Americans are yet aware of this fact. But a growing proportion of the informed public is not merely conscious of it but is increasingly alarmed at what it portends. America's continued social and economic progress is now seriously endangered by the sharp division of its metropolitan complexes along racial lines.

HOUSING AND NEIGHBORHOODS: THE PHYSICAL AND ECONOMIC COSTS

During the postwar era the United States government has authorized almost five billion dollars of federal funds to renew and redevelop decaying neighborhoods. The bulk of these neighborhoods were occupied largely by Negroes, and segregation and the pressures it created were dominant factors in their decline. Local and state governments have contributed many hundreds of millions more to renewal and redevelopment programs. Further, while there is no estimating the monetary cost to both Negro and white families who have been victimized by speculators feeding upon racial panic, it may well be even greater than the total price taxpayers have paid for urban renewal. And this is to say nothing of the psychological and social costs.

Historically, the restriction and concentration of racial minorities into limited neighborhoods has been a prime cause of housing blight.[1] Few things are more instrumental in the deterioration of a housing unit than too many people crammed into too little space. Because exploitation flourishes wherever people are denied free choice, segregated residential patterns also tend to contribute to the exacting of excessive prices for inferior housing, and to faltering maintenance as well. This has been especially true for rental units: landlords in Negro areas have long been notorious for practicing "slumlordism" in its most extreme forms.

Negro landlords are not much less likely to engage in such exploitative practices than whites. The general framework of market restrictions encourages exploitation. Any inherent sympathy toward individuals of similar skin color is usually overcome by the opportunity to profit from their disadvantage. The availability of a "captive market" seems to undo the humanitarian feelings of most people who deal with it. Or perhaps such a market simply attracts a disproportionate number of persons devoid of ordinary human scruples.

Under ghetto conditions, even legal efforts to assure decent housing through the enforcement of housing codes face the most severe obstacles. Despite claims by some groups that unequal treatment of Negroes would end if Negroes controlled their own property, it seems clear that exploitation will continue so long as the larger restrictions of residential segregation remain.

In Washington a special study by the District of Columbia government showed that in 1960, despite great improvement in the housing situation of Negroes, overcrowding remained four to five times as frequent for the city's nonwhite households as it did for its white households. The problem was especially severe for those nonwhites who rented their dwellings, *even at the highest income levels.* At incomes of $10,000 and more, more than one-fourth of nonwhite rented households were overcrowded.[2]

Though nonwhite homeowners in general fare considerably better than do nonwhite renters, they also fare considerably less well than white owners. Often the only housing they are allowed to buy is old and in poor condition. Many families undertake extensive repairs and renovations soon after assuming ownership, and the results can be observed in the improved maintenance of many neighborhoods that Negroes have entered in recent years. But some Negro families are forced to pay prices so exorbitant that they have little money left with which to keep up their properties. Moreover, monthly housing costs often are increased by extortionate financing arrangements — such as "lease-purchase" plans or high interest rate second and third mortgages — which Negroes must accept because "reputable" mortgage lending institutions either refuse their business outright or are unwilling to lend money on properties priced at the inflated levels many Negroes must pay. In all too many cases, usurious costs are incurred because the properties available to Negroes are in the hands of speculators who insist on profiting outrageously not merely from the sale itself but from the financing as well.

Exploitation in such a "rigged" market largely accounts for the important finding, in several carefully conducted studies, that Negro entry into a neighborhood does not necessarily send its real estate prices plunging downward; indeed it often causes them to *rise* instead. The most thorough of these studies, *Property Values and Race,* conducted for the Commission on Race and Housing by the noted economist Luigi Laurenti,[3] surveyed 10,000 transactions in all. The author found that prices rose in 44 percent of cases when Negroes entered, remained stable in another 41 percent, and declined in only 15 percent. These were *long-term* trends, and they were measured *relative to trends in carefully matched neighborhoods which remained all white.*

It does not follow from this that the relatively higher prices of homes in many racially changing neighborhoods benefit the white families who leave them. Rather, the money often goes into the pockets of the speculators who have helped panic the whites into selling for *less* than their homes would bring on a "free" or open market situation. The speculators then proceed to resell the homes to Negroes (often in a matter of days) for *more* than their normal market value.[4]

The Laurenti study found chaotic price fluctuations in many of the neighborhoods it investigated—presumptive evidence both of racial panic and the success of sharp operators in exploiting it. Technically speaking, these blockbusters represent an unscrupulous minority of the real estate industry—"outlaws" in a moral if not a legal sense. But their activities would not be profitable if the set of restrictions created by segregation were not accepted by the large majority of builders, brokers, and lenders—not to speak of large segments of the white public as a whole.

By adroitly holding back the Negro market, and permitting its housing needs to be satisfied only on a "waiting list" basis, reputable bankers and members of the building and real estate industries have contributed to the conditions under which their not-so-scrupulous colleagues can flourish. Working in tandem with the speculators, such individuals assiduously guard against the entry of Negroes into solidly white areas of the city. In testimony recently given before the Commissioners of the District of Columbia, the president of the Mortgage Bankers Association of Metropolitan Washington bluntly stated that "applications from minority groups are not generally considered in areas that are not recognized as being racially mixed."[5] A study by the Chicago Commission on Human Relations found that such a policy was pursued by almost all lending sources in that city.[6] Voluminous evidence from both social research surveys and testimony before legislative and executive bodies indicates that the same is true of real estate boards in cities throughout the country.

The profits to be derived from such speculative real estate activities is suggested by a study conducted in Philadelphia. Chester Rapkin and William G. Grigsby, two highly respected real estate economists, found that speculators operating in changing areas double their investments, on the average, in less than two years. For such profits to a very few individuals, the whole community pays heavily.[4]

If the Negro ghettos continue under the same rigid restrictions as at present, conditions are likely to become worse rather than better in the near future. The products of the postwar "baby boom" are now reaching maturity and forming families of their own; they will continue to do so throughout the late 1960's and early 1970's. The Negro housing need will contribute greatly to increasing the pressures of demand which help exploitation to flourish.

HOUSING AND NEIGHBORHOODS: THE HUMAN COST

But the costs to white and Negro homeowners and to neighborhoods cannot be assessed in economic terms alone. At least as important are those costs which fall in the psychological realm — mental stress, misery, loneliness, the personal loss of being forced to leave a home and neighborhood one has grown to love. No dollar tag can be placed on such factors.[7]

Many of the neighborhoods newly entered by Negroes since World War II have been occupied by middle-aged or retired white families, who often look upon their homes there as being their last, and whose emotional attachment to both house and neighborhood is based upon ties of familiarity and friendship built up over many years. Upon the entrance of a Negro family, these occupants see themselves caught between two equally dismaying possibilities. To leave the neighborhood means breaking familiar ties and moving to a new and strange, perhaps frightening, section of the city. But to stay means coping with a situation that is just as new and strange.[8] Rapid population change tends to tear apart the social fabric of a neighborhood, destroying the informal controls which have operated against anti-social activities. Increases in crime and juvenile delinquency appear—not so much as a consequence of the activities of the residents themselves (most criminals, in fact, practice their trade elsewhere than in their own neighborhood), but because ordinary citizen vigilance no longer exists. Even the physical structures of the neighborhood may undergo marked change, if the transition is sufficiently quick and complete. Well-kept, single family homes or carefully maintained apartment houses may become tenements, rooming houses, or worse.

The effects of population changes are particularly sad

in the case of ethnic neighborhoods where much of the community's life has centered around a house of worship, and where neighbors often include kinfolk as well as friends. In such cases the change is harmful not only to individual families but to institutions and social organizations that can rarely survive transfer to another location.

It is hardly surprising that white residents of some neighborhoods have tried to resist Negro entry by acts of violence. Interestingly, these outbreaks often have occurred in neighborhoods of lower- and lower-middle incomes, particularly where the ethnic composition was predominantly Italian or Eastern European. But it is probably an oversimplification to conclude, as many observers have, that this combination of economic and ethnic factors is sufficient to explain the violence. Several middle-income communities of very heterogeneous composition—such as Levittown, Pennsylvania—have witnessed similar outbreaks.[9]

Probably the prime factor in determining whether a neighborhood will react with violence to Negro entry is the degree of threat, real or fancied, that this change poses to the white homeowners, in terms both of their financial investment and, perhaps even more important, of their stake in the social structure of the community. At the time of the violent outbreak in Levittown, Pennsylvania, for example, overbuilding and a local economic depression had combined to make houses in that community virtually unsalable. A growing number of residents were losing their homes through foreclosure proceedings. The house that was purchased by the first Negro family had been on the market for over a year. Consequently, it was sold to nonwhites at a price considerably lower than its original cost plus the cost of improvements made during the four years since it had first been offered to an exclusively white market. (This situation, of course, was a distinct departure from the typical pattern.) In these circumstances, neighboring white families reacted to Negro entry in a manner motivated not merely by fears of anticipated ill effects but

37

also by an already existent financial threat. The resulting turmoil made world-wide headlines.

In other cases, residents of ethnic neighborhoods have responded similarly when they saw themselves threatened with the loss of community values they held dear. It must be noted, however, that violence probably would not have occurred in any of these neighborhoods if the initial Negro entrant had been viewed as an individual homeseeker rather than as the precursor of an invasion.

Residential segregation has probably been a factor in more racial disturbances than is commonly realized. One disturbance where housing segregation may have been an important "hidden" cause, was the 1964 Mummers' Parade in Philadelphia. This parade is an annual New Year's Day event of national note. The Mummers, which excludes Negroes from membership, is a confederation of all-white ethnic clubs situated largely in foreign-origin neighborhoods of south Philadelphia. In recent years some of these districts have been under heavy pressure from the spreading Negro "ghetto."

It had been a long-time tradition of the parade for several of its groups to appear in blackface. The practice was gradually dying out when, late in 1963, several Negro organizations demanded its immediate and total discontinuance. The Mummers refused. To avoid possible riots, the mayor ordered the parade postponed, and finally the Mummers backed down. Some observers believe that the Mummers would not have clung so adamantly to a practice clearly offensive to many of their fellow Philadelphians had they not deeply resented the "encroachment" of these citizens upon neighborhoods they regarded as their own.

Again, in a special report on the "race riots" that erupted in a number of American cities in the summer of 1964, FBI chief J. Edgar Hoover ascribed the disorders in Negro slums less to racial factors *per se* than to the miserable dwellings and neighborhood conditions in which most of the rioters were forced to live—conditions which in part are the product of racial discrimination and the exploitative practices that follow in its wake.

Until that time when ghetto areas are reduced and eventually eliminated, racial tensions in America's metropolitan areas are likely to continue and to grow. They will be generated both by the conditions within the crowded ghetto areas themselves, and by the apprehensions of surrounding white residents as the Negro areas expand inexorably outwards.

IMPACT UPON PUBLIC POLICIES AND PROGRAMS

The damage caused by residential segregation is not limited to neighborhoods. Segregation affects entire cities and their surrounding metropolitan communities, and, indeed, the nation as a whole. It has a devastating impact upon many public policies and programs at the local, state, and even national level, and its effects lead to large public expenditures that otherwise would not be needed or could be used elsewhere. More significantly, it sometimes frustrates the implementation of public decisions or warps the results of governmental programs, subverting the intent of the framers.[10]

While segregation is by nature a localized phenomenon, its broad public effects are not. As America becomes more and more heavily urbanized—perhaps the more fitting term is "metropolitanized"—more and more of the problems associated with segregation require the assistance of the federal government. Education, housing, urban renewal, welfare, labor, even highways—these are only some of the major areas of federal activity where segregation today has marked effects.

The Hindrance to Equal Opportunity. While recent national progress toward securing equal rights for minority groups in regard to schools, employment, housing, public facilities, and voting privileges represents a great step forward, civil rights measures alone no longer are sufficient. The expansion of segregated living patterns has created a paradoxical situation in which legal guarantees, however systematically enforced, often have only a minimal effect. The sheer massing together of minority populations has sharply undercut the practical significance of such guarantees.

A case in point is the attempt to create equal educational opportunities for all races by legal fiat alone. In its 1954 decision declaring segregation in public education unconstitutional, the Supreme Court held that racially segregated schools were inherently unequal in the opportunity they provided students of different races. But ten years after that momentous decision, segregated schools are still the order of the day—not only in the South, against whose policies the decision was chiefly directed, but, more significantly, in large parts of the North and West as well. What is more, most of the major Northern cities had been opposed to segregated public education even before the Court's decision. Leaving Southern recalcitrance to one side, the entirely new problem that confronts urban areas outside the South is to maintain integrated schools in the face of swiftly changing populations.[11]

For a vivid illustration of this problem, let us again look at Washington, D.C. At the time of the Supreme Court decision, Washington, which geographically is located among the border states, had a completely segregated educational system. Once the Court announced its decision, the city desegregated its schools immediately. Yet now, only a decade later, the school system once again is almost entirely segregated. "Resegregation" is the term some concerned local citizens have coined for this disturbing phenomenon.

The major cause of "resegregation" is to be found in the characteristics of Washington's population, both white and Negro.[12] In 1960, while about 55 percent of the *total* population was nonwhite, almost 75 percent of the *school-age* population and almost 80 percent of the *public school enrollment* was nonwhite. The difference between the latter two figures is accounted for by white children who attended private institutions. But the more significant and larger disparity between the first two figures—between the percentage of nonwhites in the total population and in the school-age population—is explained by the fact that the Negro residents have far more children than do the whites. Children under fifteen made up more than one-third of the city's Negro population but less than one-sixth of the white population.

This difference, as we have seen, is not explained by popular notions about Negro fertility. We have already noted that the fertility rates of whites in some of the newer Washington suburbs were in fact much higher than were those of Negroes living in the city. It is explained rather by the great suburban exodus of young child-bearing white families.

Between 1950 and 1960 the *only* numerical increase for whites within the city of Washington occurred in the category over sixty years of age. By 1960 about half of all whites in Washington, and about two-thirds of the city's white *adults,* were past the age of forty. By contrast, the Negro population of Washington was much more "normal"—containing children, working-age adults, older people, and the spectrum of families in about the same proportions as in the nation as a whole. This proportion is the main cause of Washington's "'resegregation," a phenomenon that can be seen in less extreme forms in many other cities as well.

Developments like resegregation often have side effects that tend to reinforce the impact of their initial consequences. For example, the disproportion of Negro youngsters in the schools resulting from the migration of young white families probably generated an even further exodus among those families who might not object to school integration *per se* but still did not wish to see their children be a minority in primarily Negro classrooms. It is in such ways that segregation feeds upon itself and creates built-in obstacles to its elimination.

How can Negro slum children be given equal educational opportunities today in America's great cities, where their frequent deficiencies of background and home environment cannot even be leavened through contact with children who have been more fortunate? The answer is now being sought in experimental educational programs costing millions of dollars—which, if they are successful, will ultimately mean the spending of many billions more as the programs are extended to all those who need them. This cost is but a small part of the price we eventually will have to pay to undo the effects of segregation. And for the immediate future, there remains the basic question of whether or not the programs will work, given the tremendous environmental obstacles they confront.

The Hindrance to Rational Planning for Growth and Change. As indicated in the first chapter, America must plan carefully if it is to be able to absorb future population growth without sacrificing the beauty and spaciousness which have so long been valued by its citizens, and if it is to deal successfully with such by-products of its own technological achievement as automobile traffic, pollution, and urban "sprawl." Planning is necessary, also, if America is to eliminate physical blight generated in part by segregation, and human blight caused by denying individuals the opportunity to develop their full potential or by pushing their energies in the direction of socially destructive actions.

Rational planning is hampered in many ways by the factor of race. In the first chapter, we noted some of the racial implications of Washington's "Year 2000 Plan." This "plan," as currently conceived, though it responds to many of the city's problems, can extend segregation far into the future.

Another more general example in which rational planning is frustrated by the racial configuration of a city concerns the urban expressways being planned or under way in many cities as a device to help alleviate one of the many undesirable by-products of suburban growth—the excessively long commuting time between the central city and its outlying districts. Often these expressways are designed to pass through the heart of the Negro "ghettos." Because of blight, property in these areas can usually be acquired under condemnation proceedings at relatively low costs. In addition, the federal program subsidizing expressway construction offers a convenient means by which to demolish unsightly slums at minimum cost to the local community.

In more and more cities, plans for such construction are running into serious political obstacles—first, from many slum residents, who realize that the development of the highway will result in an even more seriously inadequate supply of housing; and second, from residents of better neighborhoods nearby, who recognize that demolition of the slum properties may create destructive pressures upon their own sections of the city. The resulting choice—between crippling traffic jams and a possible further loss in the more economically capable population of the cities—is not an easy one.

Still another example of the way racial segregation thwarts planning can be found in a situation that just now is beginning to take shape. In some parts of the nation, large and comprehensively planned "new towns" may soon begin to replace the spread of suburban sprawl. Many of these new communities will be planned and built from the outset as complete towns, with a full panoply of shopping, employment, and recreation facilities. The best of the new towns will also contain a comprehensive selection of different types of homes, ranging from large single houses to small apartments, so that residents will be able to satisfy their changing needs and desires without moving from the community. Walking to work and to shopping—almost a forgotten convenience in today's suburbs—will again become not only possible but easy.

Already popular in Europe and Great Britain, the new town concept offers important advantages over the sprawl that characterizes America's postwar suburban development—advantages that accrue not merely to the residents of the towns but to the entire nation. The new towns offer a way of comfortably accommodating population growth while conserving irreplaceable green space. Since many of the residents can work within the town itself and all can shop within a short distance of their homes, automobiles once more are likely to become primarily vehicles of pleasure rather than of necessity. The proliferation of multimillion dollar superhighways can be slowed down; pollution of the air by exhaust fumes will be reduced; speedy, economical mass-transit systems, now virtually out of the question in many areas because of the low density and the wide area spread of suburban growth, will become a practical possibility by which to transport residents between the compact new communities and the central cities.

But the new towns, hopeful as the prospect seems to be, are also confronted by the ever-present spectre of race. To be successful, the comprehensively planned nature of the towns calls for a more or less complete cross section of the population, in terms of incomes, family sizes, and skills. The towns will require a large number of service workers, including manual laborers, domestics, custodians, and sales people, to mention only a few categories. In many areas the only significant reservoir of workers available for many of these occupations today is the Negro population. Yet in most instances the new towns will be located too far from central cities for easy and economical commuting. Thus, in all likelihood, the workers will have to be housed in the towns themselves, if the service needs of the community are to be met at all.

But on what basis? Will the new towns contain, from the outset, pre-planned ghettos? If not, how is integration to be accomplished, given the differential income levels of the people involved and the many problems connected with providing low-cost housing under private auspices? Even if this last obstacle is overcome—as might be possible through some of the provisions of the housing bill recently enacted by Congress—will white Americans long conditioned to spatial separation, not only of races but of economic groups, accept any other arrangement?

Alternatively, let us suppose that the new towns make no provision for a complete cross section of population—which is the case with most of those now under way. Quite apart from the inconveniences and high costs which their affluent inhabitants may suffer as a result of the scarcity of service personnel, what will happen to the central cities if these glossy new towns draw away more and more of the cities' affluent residents (most white but including a few Negroes), while providing no comparable outlet for the growing population of low-income Negroes? Will "low-income" new towns then be planned for this population, thus extending the patterns of racial segregation—not only separate but grossly unequal—on a scale even now undreamed of?

These are the kinds of problems with which some of the more farsighted of the nation's urban planners and housing experts are now wrestling. Unfortunately, the number of such troubled observers does not constitute a large percentage of either the many technicians now entrusted with planning decisions or the officials and private citizens who influence housing policy at the national as well as the local level.

The Hindrance to the War Against Poverty. The United States is now committed to a total effort to eliminate poverty among its citizens—a goal to which the richest country in the world may aspire with some hope of success, but one which is by no means within easy grasp. For, as many Americans now realize, a major part of the "poverty problem" is a result of racial discrimination—focused in the expanding Negro ghettos at the heart of most American cities.

It is not easy to eliminate the accumulated ill effects of

45

denying equal opportunity to Negroes in the areas of education and work. It is even harder to deal with such problems when their victims are so concentrated geographically that the resulting demoralization and social difficulties become self-reinforcing; when, to use a simile which is less farfetched than it may at first appear, a critical mass produces a chain reaction that can only be controlled, let alone eliminated, with almost insuperable effort.

We have already touched upon one way that segregation hinders the national attempt to eliminate poverty in our discussion of the hindrances to achieving equal opportunity in education. But there are other dilemmas, no less perplexing. How, for example, can we equip youngsters to establish stable and harmonious patterns of family life when they have grown up in the everyday presence of parental desertion, illegitimacy, prostitution, and experiences with even less savory names? How can we help such youngsters to become responsible citizens and workers when their childhood has been spent in the company of persons made irresponsible beyond hope of cure by generations of hopelessness?

Legions of social workers have struggled with these problems over the years; yet the problems remain. It is by no means certain that the vast new anti-poverty programs are yet equipped with the techniques needed to solve them. The outcome is still in doubt, even though these programs express for the first time a *national* commitment to eliminate human deprivation and distress, and, consequently, larger resources than ever before, in terms of both money and personnel, will be allocated to achieve this end.

The prime focus of the new programs, in urban areas at least, is the central-city ghetto. Here the programs will provide a variety of services depending on the locality and the need: job training, especially for young people and unemployed heads of families (few of the programs as yet contain provisions assuring that the newly trained will get jobs); counseling in homemaking, budgeting, and consumer practices; legal aid to assist poor families in protecting themselves against the exploitative techniques of loan sharks and unscrupulous landlords; day care for the children of working mothers; and so forth.

Anti-poverty programs place particularly strong emphasis on improved education. In Washington, D.C., for example, the major Negro slum will have a "model school system" which its designers hope will provide educational opportunities approximating those in the best suburban schools by using new educational techniques as well as more and better teachers and smaller classes.

None of these ideas is new; many of them have been tried, with varying success, under the auspices of settlement houses or voluntary social service agencies, or even, on occasion, by some enlightened city governments. The fact that they have not eliminated poverty may be due to one of two reasons: either to inadequacies in the techniques themselves or to inadequacies in their implementation. The programs have always existed on a pitiably small scale, and so their worth has never really been tested. At best, they provide slum residents with the kinds of services which would readily be available to them (or, to a degree, would be needed less) if they were fortunate enough to be able to take their place beside those who have migrated in the past two decades to the new white middle-class suburbs. But is this enough?

If the War Against Poverty succeeds, it will in all probability not be by any magical new wonder weapon — although there is always the outside chance of a dramatic technological breakthrough such as those which revolutionized the physical and biological sciences. Victory in this war is most likely to come as it has come in most wars: through the might of superior resources or through the use of a superior strategy that effectively deploys the available resources against the enemy.

In the urban War Against Poverty, this "enemy" consists basically of the slum ghetto and the powerful forces that have produced it. The ghetto psychology, permeated as it is by a sense of hopelessness and entrapment, must somehow be transformed so that this part of the population can take its place in the mainstream of a free and open society. Simultaneously, the society itself must become truly free and open. The factors which now deny full participation to all citizens alike are, in many cases, exactly those factors which have helped create the ghettos in the first place— inequality of opportunity in jobs and schooling (which makes for inequality of preparation when improved opportunities arise) and the pressures that prevent free movement beyond the ghetto into the larger society.

The point here is that the major weakness of many current anti-poverty programs is precisely that they propose to focus themselves almost entirely *within* the ghetto. Their major emphasis is on increasing the abilities and economic chances of ghetto inhabitants through better schooling, job training, counseling, and various other special services, and on preventing the ghetto from exploding into violence. What is not yet being done on a large scale, but may prove to be absolutely essential, is to mount a major attack upon the social forces that have brought the ghetto into being and that continue to maintain it.

There is much talk to the effect that an important objective of the War Against Poverty is to change "the system" that keeps the poor in subjection. This is to be accomplished, ostensibly, largely by bolstering and mobilizing the meager powers of the poor themselves. Little is said about a direct attack upon the barriers in the larger society—"the system" itself. Few of the current urban anti-poverty programs even propose to move beyond the boundaries of the central city into the wider metropolitan area, where the barriers chiefly exist and where many of the solutions to poverty must ultimately be sought. Fewer still actually do so.

If this war is to be fought on the "enemy's" own terms, without striking decisively at his base of power, then its ultimate effect seems destined to fall short of complete success. For example, even if it should prove possible to raise the standards of slum schools to those of non-slum schools, youngsters returning home from class will still be forced to detour around drunks and junkies, pimps and pushers. For however much the chances of many are improved, in the conditions of the ghetto some will remain who are beyond hope, and their hopelessness will continue to be a potent source of the very ills the War Against Poverty hopes to root out. It may be that to eliminate them the ghetto itself will have to be rooted out.

In a very real sense, the "troops" in this war are the residents of the Negro ghettos. Few more demoralized armies have ever existed. Some observers are fond of pointing out that past ghettos in America, despite their physical shortcomings, had often been a source of unity and strength. But there are important differences between today's ghettos and those of the past, the most significant being that the older ghettos, of the Italians and the Jews, for example, bad as they may have been in many physical respects, never lacked the critical elements of hope. After all, their residents had in a sense come to them willingly, usually from worse places, with the expectation of building a better life for themselves and their descendants. This hope, moreover, was usually realized within a span of two generations at most. But for too many Negroes the ghetto has not really been an alternative—merely the only place available, and not one which perceptibly offered a path to anything or anywhere better.

The War Against Poverty must offer a way out—some hope of escaping not only poverty and the squalid living conditions which characterize its chief habitat, but also the psychological burden imposed by confinement within ghetto walls. The Negro poor must be afforded the hope not merely of bettering their own situation within the ghetto but of leaving the ghetto itself for a better place. Unless this is done, the victories in that war are likely to be short-range ones at best. Most inhabitants of the Negro slums will probably sink further into apathy once their fears are confirmed that, unlike other Americans, for them there is no escape.

IV. THE UPSURGE OF CIVIC CONCERN: GOVERNMENTAL POLICY

Housing segregation in the United States may be described aptly as a "problem in flux." In response to increased patterns of segregation in many communities throughout the nation has come a rising tide of citizen concern, expressed not only in private action but in public policy.

In the years immediately following World War II, the ranks of those opposed to discriminatory practices and racially segregated residential patterns were limited to a handful of individuals. Their attitudes were clearly out of tune with the rest of the nation's. Few laws or policy directives at either the federal or local level forbade discrimination in any segment of housing. Indeed, public policy generally encouraged segregation and condoned discriminatory practices as a legitimate means of achieving it.

Officials who opposed these practices found themselves going against the grain of prevailing law and sentiment. Private groups who proposed the creation of non-discriminatory housing developments received short shrift both from the government and their fellow citizens. And some organizations, including several labor unions, which were opposed in principle to discrimination and segregation, were reluctant to translate their policy statements into effective practice for fear that their rank-and-file membership would not support it. Their reluctance should cause small wonder. Until 1948 an individual homeowner who sold or rented his property to a member of a racial or ethnic minority could, under certain circumstances, be fined or even jailed for his action.[1]

Today, in contrast, thousands of Americans across the nation are actively and openly participating in organizations whose announced purpose is to desegregate residential areas. In 1963 the National Committee Against Discrimination in Housing identified nearly three hundred voluntary citizen committees working for integration in housing in their respective communities; by mid-1965 the number was estimated at more than 1,000 private groups. Dozens of fair housing groups now ring such major cities as Boston, New York, Philadelphia, and Washington, aimed at opening up the suburbs around each.[2] Inside these cities, other groups are working both at the neighborhood level and on a city-wide basis to prevent racial panic and to promote racial stabilization in neighborhoods entered by Negro families. Nearly all of the nation's major religious bodies and labor unions have committed themselves to policy statements advocating residential integration, and they increasingly have translated their verbal commitments into positive action.

As of July, 1965, twenty states and the District of Columbia had laws on their books barring discrimination in at least part of their housing supply. In sixteen states plus the District of Columbia, the laws were quite comprehensive and covered a substantial portion of all private housing. Taken together, the states with comprehensive coverage contained about eighty million people, or 44 percent of the total population of the United States at the 1960 census. Thus, by the mid-sixties nearly half the citizens of the country were living in communities where public policy was clearly opposed to deliberate segregation on the basis of either race, creed, color, or national origin, even in housing built under private auspices.[3]

At the national level, federal housing policies have taken a similar turn, moving from official sanction of segregation to the 1962 Presidential Order which bars discrimination in any housing that receives federal assistance. This drastic reversal of public policy and private practice—a change of almost revolutionary dimensions—occurred in a span of no more than a decade and a half. And the change was accomplished not through violence or political disorder but within the constitutional system of judicial, legislative, and executive action and through the individual freedoms that form the basis of American society.

FEDERAL HOUSING POLICY: THE EARLY YEARS

To understand this dramatic change in public policy it is necessary to review a bit of history. Large-scale federal involvement in the housing field began during the depths of the post-1929 depression, when mortgage foreclosures were widespread and the supply of jobs vastly inadequate to the demand. Government involvement was prompted chiefly by these economic considerations. It sought to salvage private home ownership and stabilize credit and real estate values, and to expand the volume of residential construction, thereby creating additional jobs to counter the economy's downward spiral.[4] The oldest of the current federal housing agencies, the Federal Housing Administration, established by the Housing Act of 1934, was created to insure residential mortgages on private dwellings against the failure of the individual borrower to repay. Similarly, the principal objective of the experiments in low-rent public housing undertaken about this time was to provide work for the unemployed. Creating decent shelter for poorly housed families was only a secondary consideration.

In a short while, however, additional legislation in the area of housing began to aim at social as well as economic goals. The Housing Act of 1937, which created the predecessor of today's Public Housing Administration, sought to develop good housing for low-income families. Twelve years later, the Housing Act of 1949 stated that the goal of American housing policy was to provide "a decent home and a suitable living environment for every American." None of this is to say, of course, that economic considerations do not remain today at least as important as social ones in determining federal action.

Early federal action in the area of housing was based primarily on what the experts of the time thought was economically sound practice. Most of these experts (though not quite all) believed that the goal of economic stability dictated neighborhoods that were homogeneous in terms of social class and race and that would remain so in perpetuity. As erroneous and unrealistic as this belief now appears, it nonetheless was widely accepted then.

Thus, at the outset, the power of the national government was set against open housing for all its citizens. Not only did federal programs condone discriminatory practices in the housing field, they actively encouraged and at times even required them. The Federal Housing Administration's *Underwriting Manual* referred to "inharmonious racial or nationality groups" and advised appraisers to lower the rating of properties in mixed neighborhoods, "often to the point of rejection." The manual stated: "If a neighborhood is to retain stability, it is necessary that properties shall continue to be occupied by the same social and racial group." To this end, the FHA provided a model racial restrictive covenant which it recommended be included in property deeds.[5]

54

Private developers who sought to market their housing to all financially qualified persons, regardless of race, thus were discouraged from doing so. Federal officials, perhaps wary of being found in violation of the Fourteenth Amendment's guarantee of equal protection under the law, did not always tell developers in so many words that they would not be granted mortgage insurance to build for interracial occupancy. Instead, the government often employed a variety of delaying tactics which prevented such building programs from getting under way. Some failed financially as a result; other developers simply gave up on their objective and accepted the requirement of segregation.[6]

During this same period the Public Housing Administration, established to assist the construction of housing for low-income families, recognized the need for housing among minority groups by a "racial equity" formula which required "equitable provisions for eligible families of all races determined on . . . their needs." Whether such provision was to be on a segregated or integrated basis, however, was left to local discretion. Almost invariably, choice came down on the side of segregation. This meant that units were allocated to whites and nonwhites in proportions that were (at best) equitable at the time the housing was first built, and which could not readily be altered when the relative needs of the two groups changed.[7]

These policies held firm altogether for some fifteen years, from 1935 to 1950—a period during which about fifteen million new dwellings were constructed. Of the impact of this era, the well-known housing expert Charles Abrams has written:

> Federal housing agencies pursued a concerted, relentless, and officially sanctioned drive to keep people living only near their own kind and to get them to oppose intrusions by anybody who was different. Federally approved racial covenants soon covered the greater part of suburbia; neighborhoods were divided into

55

those of the elite and the unwanted; and intolerance gained such rapid headway that men in high national office now saw nothing wrong in signing restrictive covenants, one of the most popular of which barred not only Negroes, but Jews, Armenians, Persians and Syrians.[8]

In the early 1940's Gunnar Myrdal, the eminent Swedish economist who was then examining America's racial problems, wrote: "Government policies have, on the whole, served as devices to strengthen and widen rather than to mitigate residential segregation."[9] This criticism was to remain valid for at least a decade after he wrote it. And in some respects, as we shall see, it is still unfortunately true today.

THE TURNING POINT: 1948

The turning point in federal policy toward residential segregation came in 1948, when the Supreme Court ruled that restrictive racial covenants in regard to private property were legally unenforceable. Until that year the judiciary could, and frequently did, declare a sale in violation of such a covenant null and void. The seller could be sued for damages, fined, or even jailed. In its 1948 decision, however, the Court held that enforcement of such covenants represented discriminatory action by the state and hence was in violation of the Fourteenth Amendment.

While this decision did not rule out the right of individual citizens to make *voluntary* private agreements among themselves, it nonetheless meant that any owner who wished to *disregard* racial covenants could now do so without fear of legal retaliation. Since 1948 many have, with the result that a number of minority families have been able to enter neighborhoods from which they once could have been excluded by law.[10]

The first official reaction of the Federal Housing Administration to the Court's decision was to declare the decision inapplicable to its own operations. Although the agency removed from its manual both its model covenants and its references to neighborhood homogeneity, it continued to insure mortgages with racial restrictive covenants. Finally, late in 1949, the agency yielded and declared that after February 15, 1950, it would no longer do so. The Veterans Administration, which since the war had provided mortgage guarantees for veterans, and the Urban Renewal Administration, established by the Housing Act of 1949 to facilitate urban renewal programs in local communities with the assistance of federal funds, both issued similar statements.

Since 1950, then, racial restrictive covenants have vanished from new developments receiving government mortgage guarantees or other federal assistance. They still remain on the books, however, in many older neighborhoods, as well as in occasional new developments that receive no direct government support. While covenants no longer can be backed by court enforcement, their continued presence is often sufficient to deter many persons from entering a neighborhood and risking the hostility of its residents.

CHANGES IN FEDERAL POLICY: 1950 - 1962

Beginning in 1950 and continuing through the next twelve years, federal housing programs in certain limited sectors of the housing supply gradually changed from passive toleration of non-segregation to active encouragement of non-discrimination and integration.

The next big change in national policy after the Supreme Court's decision came in 1951. The FHA and the VA both ruled that thereafter all insured properties acquired by them (usually under foreclosure proceedings) would be made available to all buyers or renters, without regard to race, creed, or color.

There is no doubt that these rulings have often been violated, since both agencies delegate the responsibility for marketing such properties to local real estate agents. Nevertheless, in a number of cases where a Negro family has been sophisticated enough to protest against an instance of discrimination, it has obtained satisfaction. Moreover, at least one voluntary citizen group attempting to open up housing opportunities for Negroes in the suburbs of Philadelphia has found these regulations of considerable value in its operation.[11] One should add also that—fortunately for the general welfare but unfortunately in regard to the housing of minority groups—foreclosures have been relatively infrequent in most parts of the country since World War II. (The regulations of the FHA and the VA were materially strengthened in 1959, when both agencies required that their current listings be made available to all interested persons and agencies at their local offices. Prior to this time such listings had remained a matter of private information between the local offices and private agents.)

In 1954 the FHA widened its concern. The agency's administrator instructed local offices to take "active steps to encourage the development of demonstration open-occupancy projects in suitably located key areas." Prior to this the local offices generally had opposed the efforts of developers to build for a racially mixed market, urging them instead to restrict their sales to one race or the other. In itself, the instruction from the national office probably did little to encourage open-occupancy policies on the part of builders who otherwise were opposed to them. But it no doubt made life easier for the developers who desired to build for open-occupancy, as a handful thereafter did.

Then in 1957, at the instigation of the state of New York, both the FHA and VA began signing formal agreements of cooperation with state and local agencies responsible for enforcing laws or ordinances against housing discrimination.[12] Such cooperation normally involves an exchange of appropriate information between the two agencies (including, on the part of the federal agency, regular lists of the projects it has approved, and on the part of the enforcing agencies, reports of complaints it has received charging discrimination in federally aided housing); and an agreement by the FHA or VA to inform developers of the law and their responsibilities under it and to suspend benefits to any builder whom the enforcing agency finds guilty of discrimination. The latter agreements often have proved helpful in securing compliance with state and local law. The government's Urban Renewal Administration generally follows the same policies.

In 1959 the federal government dropped the system of racial quotas it maintained in regard to housing built primarily for persons displaced by urban renewal, and in 1960 it banned discrimination in a special direct loan program to assist the elderly in meeting their housing needs.

Although these regulations and directives represented a large stride forward, they again in themselves did little to change the rigid patterns of segregation that existed in America's residential communities. As recently as 1962, close to 80 percent of all public housing projects that received a federal subsidy were occupied by only one race. Segregated projects were located as far north as Scranton, Pennsylvania, and Plattsburgh, New York—and, as might be expected, in practically every locality in the South.[13] The great bulk of new suburban housing backed by FHA and VA mortgage guarantees was occupied exclusively by white families. A scattering of developments built on urban renewal sites were made available to both Negroes and whites, but they have been limited mainly to the largest cities of the North and West, and frequently priced at or close to luxury levels. Where integration existed, it was largely due to state and local laws rather than national directives.

Nonetheless by 1962, partly as a result of these directives, it had become increasingly clear that the problems of discrimination were too interwoven with residential segregation to be solved with a few piecemeal and timid changes in federal policy or by local fiat alone.

THE PRESIDENTIAL EXECUTIVE ORDER: NOVEMBER 20, 1962

The beginning of the end in such piecemeal policy came on November 20, 1962, when President Kennedy issued an Executive Order barring discrimination in all housing that received federal aid after that date. The President was fulfilling a pledge he had made during his campaign for office:

> Let me give one example of an important immediate contribution that could and should be made by the stroke of a presidential pen.
>
> Eleven months ago the Civil Rights Commission unanimously proposed that the President issue an executive order on equal opportunity in housing.
>
> The President has not acted during this time. He could and should act now. By such action, he would toll the end of racial discrimination in all federal housing programs, including federally assisted housing.
>
> I have supported this proposal since it was made last September. The Democratic platform endorses it. A new Democratic Administration will carry it out.

The order he signed, though considerably more limited than many of its supporters had urged, and promulgated by executive rather than legislative action, nonetheless was the first explicit official statement that at the level of national policy the country was opposed to discrimination in housing.

The principal thrust of the order is twofold. It deals with

(1) property owned and operated by the federal government (mainly housing on military or other government installations and units repossessed by the FHA and VA) and (2) property which receives some form of government assistance, either through loans or other contributions (public housing, urban renewal projects, college housing, etc.) or through mortgage insurance or guarantees (FHA and VA projects). Builders and others who persisted in discriminatory practices in regard to such housing after November 20, 1962, were subject to a number of penalties, including cancellation of their contracts or even exclusion from further governmental assistance. In an effort to extend the impact of the order somewhat—since a large percentage of the total housing supply remained outside its area of control—the President included a clause directing federal housing agencies to use their "good offices" to end discrimination in the existing supply of federally aided housing.

At the end of April, 1964, almost a year and a half after the order was signed, it was estimated that about 932,000 units of housing had come under its directives. In June, 1964, it was estimated that between 12 and 20 percent of all new residential construction was covered.

But, as always, the segregation that had grown with the construction of previous years still remained. Summing up both the limitations and the value of the Executive Order shortly after it was issued, Charles Abrams wrote:

> The Executive Order will . . . touch only a small fraction of the housing market. If any real gains are to be made, its coverage must be widened or more individual state laws laboriously sought. The President's Order is no more than a small first federal step toward breaking the bottleneck in housing discrimination.

> Nevertheless, its importance cannot be discounted. First steps in civil rights legislation have often led to second steps when the will to move ahead has been present. The Order affects some parks and public fa-

cilities connected with urban renewal and will also have some value in demonstrating that builders who adopt a no-discrimination policy need not have their investments jeopardized. Moreover, since the Order authorizes "educational programs" and the use of the government's "good offices," some progress may conceivably be made by voluntary cooperation.[14]

ACTION AT THE STATE AND LOCAL LEVEL

While the federal government was moving slowly toward its policy of non-discrimination in housing, several states and municipalities were moving in the same direction—and in recent years have proceeded at a more rapid pace.[15]

Prior to 1954 only a small handful of states in the North and Midwest had legislation which barred discrimination in any segment of their housing supply. The laws usually covered only low-rent public housing and occasionally units that received such special forms of public assistance as tax exemptions or write-downs on land costs. As a rule, the laws were enforced through the judiciary, and they provided for no educational or other persuasive techniques at the executive level.

The first legislation against discrimination in FHA- or VA-aided housing was an ordinance passed by New York City in 1954; the state legislature enacted a similar bill a year later. In both cases, enforcement of the legislation was placed in the hands of a public agency already in existence whose task was the enforcement of earlier non-discrimination laws. Since then, local and state laws against housing discrimination have spread more rapidly than any preceding form of civil rights legislation.

As of mid-1965, sixteen states and a number of major cities (including the District of Columbia) have barred discrimination in a substantial portion of their private housing supply. In most instances (as in New York City and New

York State, for example) the laws cover both new and existing housing not subject to government aid. Almost all the laws go beyond President Kennedy's Executive Order both in scope and in their potential for enforcement. They cover a number of the nation's most populous industrial states, including New York, New Jersey, Pennsylvania, Massachusetts, and Michigan.

In light of the rapid rate with which such legislation has come into being, it seems clear that even had the Presidential Order not been signed it would have been only a matter of years until a majority of the American public lived under some form of legal prohibition against discrimination in housing. The Order, in essence, was merely an extension to the federal level of a principle already gaining wide acceptance in states and localities across the nation.

Beyond barring discrimination in housing, a number of states and localities have taken other steps to combat the practices which have helped engender the recent spread of segregation. Some areas have moved against the blockbusters, making it illegal for real estate agents to induce whites to sell by employing defamatory allegations about minority groups—including the oft-used myth that Negroes depreciate property values.

At the time of this writing, however, there is a cloud on the horizon. The citizens of California recently repealed by referendum at least a portion of the state anti-discrimination law after a heated campaign in which real estate interests were deeply involved both personally and financially. The constitutionality of the referendum is still in question at the moment. As we have seen in previous chapters, the repeal of such a law ultimately will work *against* the real estate industry and society as a whole, through the vast extension of the overcrowding and exploitation that inevitably will follow upon any reinforcement of discriminatory practices. It is obvious that the promoters of the California referendum, as well as those who doubtless will urge similar regressive measures elsewhere now that the California

63

campaign has been "successful," do not realize where their own best interests lie. Time will tell whether the citizenry as a whole is wiser and better informed. The passage of an anti-discrimination law covering housing by the Ohio legislature *after* the California referendum gives hope that reason will prevail.

THE LIMITS OF LAW

The mere passage of a law, or the promulgation of an order or a judicial decision, is in itself no solution to a problem as complex and widespread as is the current pattern of racial segregation.

So far, for one thing, no state or local law against housing discrimination has been backed up with the enforcement machinery it requires to be fully effective. The same is true of the Presidential Order, which is being enforced chiefly by previously existing housing agencies, with their regular staffs and unchanged structures, aided by a small President's Committee on Equal Housing Opportunity. This committee, despite its national responsibilities, has less paid staff than is available to enforce the anti-discrimination housing laws of New York State alone.

But the most important limitations of law in this field do not lie in the area of enforcement. Far more serious is the fact that any present law must be superimposed upon a set of housing policies and programs which, at their root, actually sustain segregation. The truth is that, *given the present structure and methods of federal intervention in the area of housing, even complete non-discrimination in regard to federal benefits would not greatly affect the continuing expansion of segregated patterns of residence.*

No statement as bold as this, and as sweeping in its implications, should be made without factual support. To explain and justify it, we shall have to leave our main point and look briefly at the premises and operations of the major federal housing programs.

There are three of these: FHA and VA, public housing, and urban renewal. The largest and most significant of these has been the FHA loan guarantee program, with its post-World War II parallel, the VA mortgage guarantee program for veterans (now gradually diminishing in importance). Both programs have placed the fiscal soundness of government behind the individual homeseeker (or, in the case of rental property, the builder-landlord), who thus has the benefit of longer repayment terms, lower down payments, and somewhat lower interest rates than normally would be available from private mortgage sources.

But these benefits generally accrue to individuals who meet fairly strict credit standards—standards imposed both by the governmental underwriting agency and the private lender. A certain minimum of *present* income combined with good prospects for *future* income have been paramount, coupled with evidence of faithful repayment of past obligations. Even aside from the racial discrimination that marked the early practices of these agencies, only a small percentage of Negro households could qualify at the price levels that have prevailed in new private housing since World War II.

A second feature of the FHA and VA programs bears upon the problem of segregation. Since the new housing of the postwar era has been built largely on the outskirts of the cities, these FHA and VA programs can be said to have enhanced the tendency toward white dominance in the suburbs—though this effect was largely independent of any direct racial bias in the application of the programs.

In contrast to the financial criteria employed by FHA and VA, federally subsidized public housing qualifies its tenants on the basis of maximum rather than minimum income. Under such a requirement, relatively small numbers of whites in many communities can qualify. Indeed, in some areas a substantial majority of the residents are Negro.

65

In further distinction to FHA-VA, most public housing projects have been constructed in the older central cities. But, paradoxically, the effect on patterns of segregation has been the same. Thus, while the FHA and VA in effect have been promoting white dominance in the suburbs, public housing has tended to promote Negro dominance in the cities. Certainly it has done little to disperse the ghetto concentrations.

Urban renewal, the third member of the federal housing triumvirate, was instituted to attack the problem of growing physical decay in urban core areas. In operation it has also tended to assume as an objective the attraction of white families back into the cities which they had previously deserted in large numbers to occupy the new housing made available on easy terms in the suburbs through FHA and VA guarantees. Thus, ironically, one governmental housing program is attempting to offset the effects of another.

As noted earlier, sites chosen for urban renewal most often are occupied by racial minorities. These groups, chiefly of low income, are usually displaced by housing units that are priced in the middle- to upper-income brackets. For this reason alone, regardless of possible discrimination, the housing almost invariably becomes largely or all white.

Under the law, renewal agencies must relocate the displaced families into "decent, safe, and sanitary" housing; but across the nation their procedures have come in for much criticism. Whether or not all are valid, the essential fact is that most people relocated are moved only a short distance from their former homes.[16] For example, one study found that two-thirds of the residents relocated within a radius of twelve city blocks. In this way, low-income minorities come to form residential rings around the project site. Sometimes this movement sets off a chain reaction. Whites in the neighborhoods into which the displaced move decide to take up residence elsewhere. (So, in many instances, do the more financially secure Negroes.) The ultimate effect is to create spreading waves of racial change, which in the end produce only a broader extension of segregated living patterns.

All three programs recently have made special efforts to overcome or mitigate some of their more unfortunate effects. Section 221(d)3 of the Housing Act of 1961 makes FHA-insured loans available at below-market interest rates (an indirect and limited form of subsidy) to families whose income is somewhat below the levels required for unsubsidized private housing. In the public housing program, a number of local authorities have tried to preserve a racial balance in their projects and have been experimenting with various forms of non-project housing to be distributed throughout the community. Urban renewal programs are paying increased attention to relocation procedures. They are also placing greater emphasis upon rehabilitation of existing dwellings, with "spot clearance" of only the worst units—a procedure which reduces the number of families that must be displaced.

Recently, the passage by Congress of the 1965 Housing Act has produced major additions to the techniques with which the housing agencies can work to overcome the negative effects of their efforts upon population distributions. Probably the most important is the rent-subsidy provision which will free public subsidies from some of the limitations that have been imposed upon them since the establishment of the Public Housing Administration in 1937. These supplements can offer great possibilities for change, provided they are applied with the greatest possible vision and flexibility. This, of course, will require not only federal resolve but local community support as well—matters on which more is said in Chapter Six.

V. THE UPSURGE
OF CIVIC CONCERN:
PRIVATE CITIZEN ACTION

At the same time that public policy has been moving toward the principle and practice of non-discrimination in all areas of housing, a growing number of private groups have been working in their own ways to promote residential desegregation. In some cases these groups have aimed at assuring the effective implementation of the law; in other instances their efforts have preceded legislation and have often been helpful in obtaining it.

Much of this activity is the product of local "grassroots" concern. Often it has evolved with little or no organizational support or guidance. In other instances action by private agencies has come about at the request of individual citizens or with citizen concern providing an important first step. On a few occasions the initiative has come from individual entrepreneurs in the building industry.

As with government action, private activity at first was largely piecemeal and was usually directed toward narrow and immediate goals: stemming panic among white residents in a neighborhood recently entered by Negroes, effecting a policy change in regard to a segment of the housing supply where minority needs were grossly under-supplied, or constructing and marketing a single housing development on an interracial basis as evidence that such a procedure was commercially feasible. Along with most of these efforts went attempts to change the attitudes of the white majority.

As these early programs have matured and knowledge about the dynamics of race and housing has grown, it has become increasingly apparent that success in one area may be offset by failure in another, or may not even be possible to achieve without a coordinated program directed toward several areas at once. Recently, a few of the more sophisticated and better financed of the private programs have attempted to work on two or more fronts simultaneously; or at least to coordinate their own limited activities with those of others focused on different aspects of the same problem.

The most significant private approaches to residential desegregation since the end of World War II fall into four categories: (1) the construction of new housing on an open-occupancy basis; (2) efforts to establish an integrated balance of families in neighborhoods entered by nonwhites; (3) efforts to open up new housing opportunities in areas previously closed to Negro occupancy, usually in postwar suburban communities; and (4) attempts to secure changes in public policy through legislation or executive action.

This chapter will discuss the evolution, strengths, and inherent limitations of each approach.

THE NEW PRIVATE INTERRACIAL COMMUNITY

Long before the current laws against discrimination in housing existed, a number of "intentional" communities were begun on an integrated basis.[1] The earliest known example of such a community was Penn-Craft, a depression-born cooperative in a rural area of southwestern Pennsylvania. Begun in 1937 under the sponsorship of the American Friends Service Committee (Quakers), Penn-Craft was an attempt to provide hard-pressed coal miners with the land to build their own homesteads. Five of the first fifty homeowners were Negro.

During the postwar building boom of the late 1940's and early 1950's, other developments around the country joined Penn-Craft in its non-discriminatory policy. They included a twenty-four unit rental development in St. Paul, Minnesota, constructed by one of the area's leading builders; an apartment cooperative of several hundred units in New York City; an eight-unit project of three-bedroom prefabs in a depressed neighborhood of Madison, Wisconsin; a 273-unit commercial tract of moderate-priced houses in Stockton, California; several middle- and upper-income single home cooperatives in the suburbs of Chicago, Philadelphia, and New York; and even a couple of small, Utopian communities in the deep South. By 1956 a nationwide survey located fifty such private developments, most of them situated around the heavily populated industrial centers of the North and West. Represented was every type and size of dwelling, from multi-story apartment houses to single homes on large lots, as well as every size of development, from a handful of dwellings to some that had upwards of a thousand units. Prices ran from $6,000 to $60,000.

The motives behind these early experimental communities were varied. Some were inspired by social agencies or labor unions interested in fostering racial equality, such as the aforementioned American Friends Service Committee, or the local affiliates of the National Urban League, or the United Auto Workers. Many developments were sponsored by private entrepreneurs who were interested primarily in profit and who thought that interracial occupancy would either contribute to the productiveness of their investment or at least would not hinder it. Several of the commercial developments actually were intended for all Negro occupancy but became interracial when whites found them attractive and were not discouraged from entry.

Since 1956 state and local anti-discrimination legislation has helped to bring about similar non-discriminatory policies in many more new private communities. Today housing developments which have served a racially mixed market from their inception number at least several hundred —possibly more than a thousand. A few have been opened to Negroes only as a result of litigation or by direct threat of legal action. But in the majority, compliance has been voluntary once the developer has been faced with qualified Negro applicants.

In a few areas without local ordinances barring discrimination, several new communities have been opened up to Negroes under President Kennedy's Executive Order. Exact figures are not yet available, but it seems clear that the number of such cases is quite small and represents only a tiny fraction of the housing units that receive federal assistance.

Most of the new developments marketed to an interracial clientele have been successful from both a social and a financial standpoint. Where the housing has been reasonably well constructed, located in comparatively good areas, and intelligently marketed, it has usually returned a profit to its builders and has proved generally satisfactory to its occupants, both white and Negro. Resident turnover has been as low as or lower than the rate in equivalent all-white developments nearby, and resale prices have compared favorably with others in the area. Property maintenance has generally been good.

In most cases, moreover, these interracial communities have not triggered racial changes in the neighborhoods surrounding them, nor have they produced a decline in neighboring property values. In fact, there have been a number of instances in which a well-planned and well-built interracial development has raised general property standards through the influence of its superior architecture and construction.

Such developments have made a large and important contribution to the goal of promoting equal opportunity in America's housing. Yet they contain serious limitations. In the first place, given the fact that they are private enterprises, most of the developments naturally are built for individuals who can afford to purchase or rent from profit-oriented builders. Most Negro families today cannot. This is the fault we noted in the second chapter, concerning the new housing that went up in the years after the war. Thus a majority of the residents in most of these communities have been whites, despite the fact that the developments often contain the only new housing in the area open to Negroes. The economic realities of the market situation leave no alternative. At least for the time being, then, new private interracial developments can achieve only a limited dispersion of the Negro population.

In particular, they can do nothing to relieve the housing problems of lower-income Negro families living in urban slums. Thus, while the private developments can promote some non-discrimination and integration, they cannot end segregation.

NEIGHBORHOOD STABILIZATION PROGRAMS

During the late 1940's and early 1950's several interacting factors—including the Supreme Court's ruling in 1948, the improved economic status of many Negro families, and the extreme pressure for additional living space created by the growing Negro population in the central cities—caused large numbers of Negro householders to move into white neighborhoods. These areas almost always were adjacent to dense concentrations of Negro housing, and they often represented a substantial improvement in housing quality and neighborhood amenities. As already recounted in Chapter Two, some of the neighborhoods very quickly changed from predominantly white to predominantly Negro. As time went on, however, groups of residents—both Negro and white—began to resist such wholesale changes. They formed associations to promote harmonious and stable interracial living.[2]

Probably the earliest of these postwar neighborhood stabilization programs was the Hyde Park-Kenwood Community Conference, organized in 1949 in southside Chicago. During the 1950's similar efforts were launched in Philadelphia, New York, Baltimore, Washington, and many smaller communities throughout the North.

In a typical well-organized effort, the group began by distributing educational material that stressed the advantages of the particular neighborhood with which it was concerned. This material countered some popular misconceptions about the "inevitable" effect of minority occupancy and appealed to white residents to stay calm and help the community develop peaceful and constructive modes of absorbing its new occupants. The group then would hold meetings at which both new and old residents together attempted to work out means of protecting their own and their neighbors' best interests.

As a cooperative atmosphere developed, specific stabilization techniques were put into action. Representatives of the group might be sent to talk with and ask the help of real estate brokers who were attempting to spread fear among white residents. Sometimes residents put up "Not For Sale" signs advertising their intent to remain where they were. In older neighborhoods, "clean-up, fix-up, paint-up" campaigns were organized to improve properties and stimulate neighborhood pride. Special efforts were usually made to attract additional white residents.

In many communities, stabilizing efforts have been completely spontaneous and "grass roots" in their origin. In a fewer number of instances, private or municipal agencies, organized to promote better intergroup relations, have helped to develop neighborhood programs at the request of concerned residents. In one city, Baltimore, the stabilization effort has become a city-wide program through the support of the local businessmen's group concerned with the physical and economic revitalization of the central city. In other areas—Buffalo is one—stabilization programs have become part of official urban renewal and rehabilitation efforts at the neighborhood level.

There is little doubt that a large number of these programs have accomplished what many persons formerly believed to be impossible. They have quelled panic, prevented possible violence, maintained sound property values, and brought new white families into interracial neighborhoods. Yet, like the new private interracial community, they too have their important limitations.

While stabilization efforts may prevent the excessively rapid turnover that results from panic, some annual turnover is inevitable. As homes gradually become available, they are likely to be purchased by Negroes whose demand for housing will continue to be focused on the few neighborhoods open to them. Thus, voluntary neighborhood stabilization campaigns, for the most part, are more likely to slow down racial transition and keep the change orderly than to halt it completely. As the change continues—and it is inevitable without the same kinds of tight restrictive controls which helped make the Negro ghettos what they are today—a segregated neighborhood is again likely to appear.

Indeed, it can be said that to the extent that voluntary stabilization efforts are successful in preventing wholesale racial change, they are in a sense limiting the amount of decent living space available to minorities. This is not to say that such programs are not and have not been of great value in preventing widespread anguish, unscrupulous practices, and general neighborhood deterioration. It is only to say that their value has limits, that at best they are only temporary measures to preserve individual city neighborhoods which have become open to interracial occupancy. They are holding actions until other more fundamental efforts are made to lessen discriminatory pressures throughout the whole metropolitan area.

SUBURBAN FAIR HOUSING GROUPS

Partially due to an increasing awareness of the limitations of both these programs—privately sponsored interracial developments and neighborhood stabilization efforts—a third approach to promoting residential desegregation came to the forefront during the middle and late 1950's. It sought to open up good neighborhoods far removed from the slum areas of the center city. In most cases, this meant relatively new neighborhoods in the suburbs of large cities or in the "suburban-type" areas on the edge of cities.[3]

Efforts of this sort often start with a "fair housing covenant" to which concerned citizens are asked to affix their signatures. Sometimes a donation is also requested so that an advertisement containing the covenant and its signatories can be placed in the local newspapers. The following covenant is typical. About 40,000 citizens of the northern Virginia suburbs of Washington, D.C., signed their names to it in 1965:

FAIR HOUSING STATEMENT

I believe that any person, regardless of race, religion, or national origin, has the moral right to purchase or rent a home anywhere.

I urge financial institutions, home builders, apartment owners, and real estate brokers to do business without racial or religious discrimination.

. . . .
(Signed)

If the covenant with its citizen support fails to achieve

a change of policy among local builders and real estate brokers—which, in fact, it usually fails to do—a fair housing group then often takes upon itself the task of providing real estate services on a non-discriminatory, non-profit basis. Probably the earliest "fair housing listing service" originated in Syracuse, New York, where in 1954 a group from the local Friends Meeting undertook a six-months' pilot program to bring whites willing to sell their homes on a non-discriminatory basis together with Negro families able and eager to buy good housing. In immediate, practical terms, the group had only the most limited success. Within the six-month period it effected only one transfer of real estate from a white seller to a Negro buyer. Much more important, however, is the fact that it found a broader acceptance of its program among the general public than it had hoped.[4]

In the two or three years following the Friends' pilot program, similar "listing services" sprang up in a number of other cities, including New Haven and Hartford, Connecticut; Princeton, New Jersey; Philadelphia; Natick, Massachusetts; Columbus, Ohio; and Santa Clara County, California. Quakers played a prominent part in the leadership of many of these organizations—sometimes through the offices of the American Friends Service Committee, the Quaker social service organization which operates a national Housing Opportunities Program, but often just as private citizens.

In general, the programs operated in this way: they first established a listing of whites who wanted to sell and of Negroes who wanted to buy, then tried to match the two. Along with this they often conducted an educational campaign to foster greater acceptance of the principle of non-discrimination and to smooth the way for individual minority families. In some cities a paid executive was hired to direct the program. In others it was supported almost entirely by volunteer effort, with occasional assistance from existing public or private agencies. One of the more sophisticated efforts—Friends' Suburban Housing, Inc., in suburban Philadelphia—set itself up as a commercial venture licensed under state laws to conduct real estate brokerage activities. The commercial effort was supported by a community relations program, at first largely voluntary but later guided by paid professional personnel.

In 1960 the National Committee Against Discrimination in Housing (founded in the early 1950's as an outgrowth of a successful grass-roots campaign to promote a comprehensive anti-discrimination housing ordinance in New York City) identified eighteen "independent local groups working specifically to stabilize old neighborhoods or to open new ones." By 1963 the NCDH estimated that the number had grown to at least three hundred[5]; in 1964 the committee raised its count again to five hundred local groups; and in 1965 it estimated that the number was more than 1,000.

As these groups have grown in number they have refined their objectives and coordinated their efforts with those of others in the metropolitan community. In the greater New York area, for example, some seventy fair-housing groups have joined in a federation, sharing their resources and working toward common goals. In greater Boston thirty-two fair-housing groups have formed a similar federation, which recently turned its attention to the problem of locating adequate housing for low-income families in the city's suburbs. Around Washington there are fair-housing groups in each of the major political jurisdictions in suburban Maryland and Virginia, as well as in several predominantly white neighborhoods in the northwest section of the District; their efforts are coordinated and assisted by a paid professional staff from the American Friends Service Committee's Metropolitan Washington Housing Program.

Many of these groups have achieved impressive results when seen in the light of both their limited resources and the magnitude of the restrictive patterns against which they battle. For example, in metropolitan Washington the fair-housing groups were instrumental in opening homes for more than a hundred Negro families in suburban areas of Maryland and Virginia during the first two years of their existence. This accomplishment becomes all the more remarkable given the fact that the area in which the homes were found is below the Mason-Dixon line and contains many white families who had come to Washington rather recently from homes that were considerably further south. Still more noteworthy, the entry of the Negro families was accomplished without a single significant incident of racial violence.[6]

This is not to say that none of the Negro families placed by such fair-housing listing services has felt the effects of white resentment. There have been a few serious incidents of property damage (none, however, is known of physical injury to persons), and a fair proportion of Negro pioneers has been subjected to slights ranging from cold stares to racial insults. Countering this, however, have been the efforts of the fair-housing groups to assure the new Negro residents that at least some of their neighbors welcome them. Most encouraging in this respect is the fact that a surprising number of the families report having received no overtly hostile reactions at all.

The legal basis for the work of the listing services lies in the 1948 decision of the Supreme Court. Once racial restrictive covenants were rendered unenforceable under the law, such programs could operate anywhere without fear that the residents of the neighborhoods they sought to open up could legally use a covenant to band together against them. Prior to 1948 such a response would have been virtually certain in many areas. Thus, in this instance as in a number of others, a private effort of citizens to extend the benefits of American democracy has become possible through a prior legal decision concerning an individual's constitutional rights.

The listing services perform a task of inestimable benefit, not merely to the Negroes they serve directly but to all the citizens of the metropolitan area. For once a neighborhood has been opened to a single Negro family, subsequent Negro newcomers do not face the hazards of the pioneer, and their arrival is not likely to trigger racial panic.

Morover, by scattering the Negro families they place throughout the suburban areas, the listing services open so many neighborhoods in such quick succession that the possibility of rapid racial turnover in any particular one becomes remote. As we have seen, speculators and block-busters depend heavily for their success upon the pressures created by a restricted housing supply. The fair-housing services contribute greatly to weakening the basis of their operations.

Perhaps equally important, this scattering effect also helps reduce the tendency of white families to flee from a neighborhood as soon as a Negro family enters it. When no neighborhood can be considered "safe," there is no longer any reason to run. In a number of areas where the services have been active, widespread newspaper publicity about their activities has made most white suburbanites aware of the fact that they cannot escape the possibility of Negro neighbors. While it is doubtful that all of them recognize this as a positive contribution to their peace of mind—much less as a step leading to a more stable, rational pattern of metropolitan growth—it nonetheless is both.

However, like the other approaches discussed here, the listing services offer only a limited means to eliminate residential segregation. Finding homes for over a hundred families in the first two years of operation is an impressive achievement, but when measured against the total number of Negro households in metropolitan Washington in 1960 —about 150,000—it is very small indeed. As we noted in Chapter One, the numbers of Negro families that leave the central city for the suburbs must reach the thousands every year if the expansion of the Negro ghettos is to be halted, let alone reversed. No listing service has begun to approach this figure, nor is any likely to do so in the near future.

Furthermore, any listing service, like any new private

79

real estate development with open occupancy, is confined chiefly to the more affluent segment of the Negro market—even though the income levels reached by the listing services can be somewhat lower than those served by new developments, especially in metropolitan areas where sizable older suburban sections are available at modest prices. (In Boston a listing service has received a federal demonstration grant for the purpose of opening housing opportunities in suburbs of lower-middle income.)

For all that these limitations are fundamental ones, the listing service approach is nonetheless one of the most valuable in the arsenal of private techniques combating residential segregation. For in opening a wide variety of neighborhoods previously closed to Negro occupancy, such services not only increase greatly the range of housing opportunities available to minorities but also help effect a widespread penetration of previously impervious racial barriers. And once breached, they tend to be opened for good. Altogether, these pioneering efforts lay the groundwork for a much broader dispersion of the Negro population, once resources make this possible.

PRIVATE EFFORTS TO SECURE PUBLIC ACTION

The fourth major approach of private citizens seeking to eliminate residential segregation consists of exerting political pressure in favor of anti-discrimination housing legislation and comparable governmental action. It is doubtful indeed whether most of the laws and regulations that now guard the right of all citizens to equal opportunity in housing would be on the books if not for the persistent efforts of civic interest groups.

The "grandfather" of all such citizen efforts, and the one which to this day plays a dominant role in stimulating citizen awareness of the dangers and injustices of segregation in housing, is the New York State Committee Against Discrimination in Housing—the forerunner of the National Committee Against Discrimination in Housing (NCDH) mentioned earlier in this chapter. Today, NCDH is a federation of thirty-nine religious, civil rights, labor, and civic organizations concerned with the problems of race and housing on a national level. After successfully promoting an anti-discrimination housing ordinance for New York City in 1950, the committee in only about a year succeeded in bringing a similar law into existence at the state level. While continuing thereafter to wage successful efforts to broaden and improve legislation in its home territory, the committee has also branched out to inspire similar grassroots campaigns in many other states and localities. These local campaigns have, in turn, played a major role in the proliferation of fair-housing laws at both the state and local level. In 1962 the committee spearheaded the successful campaign leading to President Kennedy's executive order banning discrimination in federally assisted housing. Through its publication, *Trends in Housing,* and through its widespread distribution of literature prepared in its own offices as well as by other organizations, NCDH has helped to provide a core of common knowledge about successful experiences and techniques in effecting housing integration.

Today the committee's programs are designed not only to provide professional service to its affiliate agencies and to the more than 1,000 local voluntary citizen groups across the nation (through its newly created Center for Fair Housing) but also to assist local, state, and federal government agencies and private entrepreneurs whose operations affect patterns of residence and the availability of housing to families of different races.

Of the four approaches discussed, this last is probably the one with greatest potential for striking decisively at the roots of the segregation problem at this point in its development. As meritorious as are the other approaches, both in stimulating grass-roots support for fair housing and in testing and perfecting adequate techniques, it is only as the concern of private citizens is translated into comprehensive public policy that fundamental change can take place.

Perhaps the major weakness of most of the efforts to date has been their narrow focus: first, their tendency to concentrate on a narrow segment of the market outside the mainstream of the Negro housing need; and second, their concentration on anti-discrimination legislation as an end in itself. This restriction of viewpoint was probably inevitable and to a certain extent desirable until quite recently. In the first place, little of value could be accomplished without the support of law to buttress the demands of individual citizens for equal rights; and second, to avoid scattering their shots the proponents of public action had first to concentrate their attention on the most economically viable segment of the Negro market.

Today, however, it is essential that the problem be placed in its larger context—as one which cannot be solved either by action affecting a particular economic level or by laws forbidding discrimination alone. It is the purpose of the next and final chapter to explore ways in which sufficiently powerful solutions may be found.

VI. BEYOND NON-DISCRIMINATION

Today the nation faces a choice. It can move forward beyond non-discrimination, beyond its attempts to provide legal guarantees of equal opportunity in the face of the enormous barriers to full equality—and go on to commit itself directly to a vigorous national effort to destroy segregated housing patterns. If the nation fails to take this crucial step, residential segregation will remain as a permanent and ever-growing part of its future.

These, then, are the alternatives which now confront Americans. There is no middle way. Anything less than an all-out campaign to end segregation decisively, once and for all, means by default that it will continue to grow.

There is still time to act, but the time is very short. As we have seen, merely to stop the continued expansion of the present Negro concentrations requires massive alteration of current population growth and movement. To eliminate the Negro ghettos entirely will require an even greater effort. Every year that action is delayed makes the task more difficult and costly to achieve — and if delayed too long, it may simply become impossible.

In earlier chapters we discussed in detail both the forces which currently are extending the ghetto complexes and the obstacles which stand in the way of eliminating these forces. Let us briefly review the basic points in this discussion.

1. The growth of segregated living patterns has attained a momentum that now tends to be self-sustaining. Most of the young families who will provide the future increase in the white population now reside outside the city. Virtually all of the young Negro families remain within it.

2. Unless this situation is promptly and decisively confronted, it may be irreversible. The baby boom of the postwar years is now reaching maturity. If the nation continues to meet the housing needs of new families as it has done in the past two decades, the next few years will see racial segregation grow to a scale dwarfing anything at present.

3. Anti-discrimination laws in regard to housing, no matter how comprehensive and how well enforced, cannot accomplish the task that needs to be done. Even if new housing were made available on an open-occupancy basis, economic barriers in conjunction with basic federal housing policies and practices would exclude most Negroes.

4. Segregation in housing makes desegregation in many other areas of society much more difficult to attain than it otherwise would be — in education (where it is almost impossible despite "busing" programs and similar arrangements); in many types of public facilities; and in employment. By impeding the efforts of Negroes to obtain equal preparation for work and life, and by hampering America's two chief racial groups from achieving a secure relationship based upon mutual understanding and respect, residential segregation thus perpetuates the social and psychological barriers that complete the vicious circle.

To attack these problems successfully will require total

mobilization and a skillful reorientation of public and private resources: first, to assure that all new housing built in the future will incorporate a balanced racial composition; and second, to encourage the maximum redistribution of population in both central cities and suburbs, so that concentrations of one race or the other are eliminated as quickly as normal real estate turnover will permit.

This is not an argument in favor of forced redistribution of population, however. Such a "solution" would run so counter to the principles of American democracy that it would not be tolerated. But force is not needed; the normal mobility of the American people has recently been so great (about half of all households moved during the latter half of the 1950's) that redistribution can be achieved through the operation of free choice, if only sufficient resources are applied to make socially desirable patterns of residence as attractive to the public as socially undesirable ones have been made in the past.

Neither do we suggest that the goal should be a rigidly planned dispersal of Negro households, so many to each square mile. This also would be neither achievable nor desirable within the American democratic framework. The goal, rather, should be complete freedom of choice in place of residence without respect to racial barriers. Within such a framework of free choice, some substantial concentrations of Negro families would doubtless remain (just as Jews have tended to congregate in certain neighborhoods even after obstacles to reside wherever they choose have been largely eliminated), but the present monolithic character of the Negro ghettos, and the social evils which they encourage, would be broken.

In the United States we often tend to underrate our own capabilities. But any objective assessment of our achievements in the two decades following the war must conclude that virtually anything we *want* to do as a nation, we *can* do. In the 1950's alone we added almost as many miles to our federal highway system as the distance to the moon. In almost every year since the end of World War II Americans built and bought over five million automobiles. We built from the ground up a vast new system for mass communication via television, establishing over five hundred local TV stations in all parts of the country, and equipping over 90 percent of the homes in America with sets.

At the same time we supported huge expenditures for national defense, while the average of our already impressive living standards rose higher and higher. Massive as it is, the problem of racial segregation cannot prevail against power like this—if the power is mobilized with vigor and decisiveness and applied with skill.

We already possess the fundamental machinery with which to attack this problem. Impressive resources exist in both public and private sectors. The need is only to harness them to the task. The basic resources are these:

1. *The panoply of governmental programs that cover housing and the physical development of urban areas.* Prime examples are the programs of the federal housing agencies. As we have seen, these programs together did much in the immediate postwar years to expand and reinforce the country's patterns of segregation. They still do so to a certain extent today. Nonetheless, if they were redirected they would be equally effective in combating and helping to erase the very trends they in part created.

Important also are the federal and state highway programs, with their potential not merely for displacing large numbers of people but also for creating avenues between homes and jobs and for promoting the commercial and industrial development of the areas through which they pass. Potentially valuable also in combating segregation are the new federal programs that seek to improve public transit, to preserve open spaces around cities and develop recreational areas, and to supplement new housing with essential community facilities.

Important subsidiary resources are the burgeoning number of local planning and zoning agencies, some of them charged with developing comprehensive plans for the growth of whole metropolitan complexes.

All such programs must determine their immediate physical objectives in the light of fundamental social goals. Otherwise the programs are likely to frustrate the best interests of the whole society.

2. *Governmental resources in the economic area.* Chief among these in terms of immediate potential is the new anti-poverty program. But there are many other federal, state, and local resources which could help overcome the economic limitations that keep Negroes in the central city ghettos and prevent them from exercising their free choice in the selection of a home and a neighborhood. Governments have massive powers to tax, to spend, and to regulate private activity in the economic sphere. While these powers are naturally exercised with discretion, they *are* brought to bear when public opinion deems it necessary. To take just one example, minimum wage laws and public welfare provisions all too often have served to keep Negroes, both those who can find gainful work as well as those who cannot, on the edge of abject poverty. Such programs can and should serve more positive ends, both for individuals and for the entire society. At present the federal minimum wage is actually below the level defined as "poverty" in the federal anti-poverty program.

No single measure would do more to destroy the economic foundations of segregation than a total mobilization of both government and private industry to produce enough jobs, at decent rates of pay, for all who need them. Action that falls short of this cannot truthfully be considered a "war" against poverty.

There is no mystery about full employment. Since World War II it has been achieved in a number of Western European nations whose political and economic systems are basically similar to our own, and whose resources are much smaller. America's defense system has for years been employed as a powerful economic stimulant for depressed areas. To construct a national program focused on peaceful ends requires only a logical extension of principles and procedures already in use. Such a program would involve both public agencies and private enterprise, the latter aided by federal incentives.

The increased incomes that would result would provide the means for many Negroes to enter the private housing market outside the slums. Even a modest rise in incomes would help a startlingly large number of families. On a national scale, for example, if the incomes of urban Negro families were boosted overall by only $20 per family per week, it would mean an increase of over 40 percent in the number with incomes over $6,000 annually. Since a very high proportion of Negro families have more than one wage-earner, this rise could be accomplished through an *hourly* average increase of considerably less than the 50 cents which the $20-per-week statistic would suggest.

3. *Governmental resources in the social area.* Social and economic measures often are closely related—as in the anti-poverty program, for example. Other programs with mixed social and economic objectives are those in the field of public education; the many welfare programs that combine counseling and social services with monetary payments; public health programs; and an array of governmental services aimed at helping people overcome the personal problems which prevent them from achieving a fully productive role in the economy and from claiming all their rights as citizens.

Not nearly as many people take full advantage of these social services as need them, and many of the programs are themselves in need of strengthening. It should be remembered, moreover, that these programs have their limits. In themselves they cannot confront the basic underlying social forces that cause poverty and segregation.

4. *Private resources.* Although public power is absolutely necessary in dealing with a problem of the magnitude of racial segregation, a multitude of important resources in the

private sector also can be brought to bear on it. Perhaps chief among them is the vast groundswell of civic and religious dismay concerning the denial of civil rights to Americans of color—a concern which so far has been focused in only a minor way on the problem of segregation in housing, and yet, as we saw in the last chapter, has achieved startling results. The grass-roots fair-housing groups represent a source of vigorous and imaginative support for the highest aims of American democracy.

Another significant resource is the private housing industry, or at least the growing segment of it which now recognizes that segregation is detrimental to its own economic objectives as well as to the long-range welfare of the whole society. Among lenders, real estate brokers, and builders, there are now a good number who voluntarily conduct their businesses on a non-discriminatory basis, even in the absence of legal prohibitions. Furthermore, most of those who have been confronted by Negro applicants under anti-discrimination laws and ordinances, even if they had opposed their enactment, have elected to comply with the law rather than challenge it in the courts.

These, then, are the available resources. How can they best be used to combat segregation? The general recommendations which follow can readily be translated into the detailed prescriptions necessitated by different laws and situations.

1. *Comprehensive planning on the federal level.* This is a crucial need. A central federal agency must have the authority to draw together programs in the areas of housing, urban renewal, highways, transportation, open-space conservation, and community facilities—and guide them toward a set of common goals.

Primary among such goals must be social objectives. Federal programs for urban development must strive actively to promote harmonious and stable relationships among the various social, economic, racial, and ethnic groups of the nation. Public actions which would tend to enhance geographic separation and economic and social divisiveness must be avoided. Federal programs must not be permitted to work at cross purposes to one another.

The Department of Housing and Urban Development at the cabinet level, enacted into existence by Congress in mid-1965, provides for the first time the basic machinery that is required. But it will not automatically achieve these ends. Strong direction will be needed in its early stages if it is not to become a counterpart of the Department of Health, Education and Welfare—which possesses a somewhat similar history but which remains to this day an essentially ungovernable combination of separate and individually powerful agencies, too often competing and conflicting.

2. *A total strategy for desegregation*—one which deploys all available resources; makes use of the best knowledge in the areas of both causes and probable solutions; keeps continually informed on the progress of its various programs; and remains flexible and subject to change as conditions warrant.

Such comprehensive planning must make maximum use of all available resources: the grass-roots fair-housing groups which have accomplished such striking results through vocal persuasion and action; the power of the law to prohibit not only discrimination but also such socially destructive practices as blockbusting and economic exploitation of the captive Negro market; the powers inherent in housing codes, planning and zoning ordinances, and the other techniques which have been developed to cope with the physical problems of urban growth; the social and economic programs which, though not directly related to segregation in housing, can help offset it—for example, fair employment and welfare programs.

The deployment of all these resources must be determined by knowledge about the social and economic obstacles which confront the geographic dispersion of minorities; about the economics of the housing market, white and Negro; about population pressures as they affect housing needs; about the other needs in the society which must be met simultaneously, including the need for jobs and for schools. A strategy for housing desegregation cannot be conceived in a vacuum; it must be thoroughly integrated with all the relevant plans and on-going activities of the society.

3. *Federal incentives for positive action.* In many fields, federal power has been applied most effectively through a set of incentives, usually financial, encouraging states, localities, and individual entrepreneurs to serve national goals. Incentives of this sort do not involve compulsion and do not infringe upon freedom of choice. Applied with vision, imagination, and flexibility (which, regrettably, is not always the case), a federal incentive program can substantially *widen* individual freedom of choice by encouraging localities and private entrepreneurs to undertake activities which ordinarily they would regard as too risky or too expensive.

In housing, for example, federal incentives have been employed to promote urban renewal (through community grants to clear slum land for redevelopment) and to promote construction of particular kinds of housing (through mortgage insurance which enables financing on liberal terms, thus broadening the market).

Incentives should now be applied to serve the objectives of comprehensive planning toward social goals. For example, incentives should make it attractive for private builders to develop complete communities which serve all economic levels and races of the population. Special incentive measures should encourage developers to incorporate from the outset a full range of community facilities, from industrial and commercial enterprises to recreational services, thus assuring (among other things) the availability of jobs for families of modest incomes. Abandoning the "bedroom" suburbs of the recent past for more adequately designed communities is another way the nation can help eliminate one-class and one-race communities.

Incentives should extend not merely to the developers but also to the market. Especially attractive terms could be offered to lure prospective buyers and renters of low to moderate income. Resettlement allowances might be provided to help with moving costs and other expenses. Again, the objective should be to promote desegregation within a framework of freedom of choice—allowing families to choose housing without the hindrances, economic and otherwise, now engendered by race.

Incentives should be applied to existing neighborhoods as well as to new communities. Since there is good reason to believe that many minority families will be reluctant to live in neighborhoods which contain few members of their own race, it is important to assure the presence of sufficient numbers through the techniques of vigorous promotion.

Further federal aid should be made available to help whole localities combat segregation. They must seek to cut across the narrow jurisdictional boundaries of municipal governments and deal with the problem in its metropolitan context.

Metropolitan planning and cooperation toward solution of *any* problem, let alone one so emotion-laden as race, has proved to be extraordinarily difficult. Thus federal incentives must be made particularly attractive. In developing them, the government must take into account the wishes of those on whose behalf they are being used.

4. *New and more flexible forms of subsidy.* If lower-income minority families are to be granted the freedom of choice in regard to housing that will permit them to disperse more widely throughout the nation's metropolitan areas, new forms of governmental housing subsidies will be necessary. Traditionally, such subsidies have been available almost exclusively for housing built by local non-profit authorities—chiefly in the form of multi-unit public "projects" which stood apart from their surroundings and massed together the less fortunate members of the popu-

lation, thereby reinforcing their disadvantages in much the same way as did the slums that the public housing was intended to replace.

More recently, however, the range of choice in subsidized housing has been widened in at least a few localities. There have been experiments with small "vest-pocket projects" which do not stand out so starkly from their surrounding neighborhoods. Existing units have also been purchased or rented by different groups at prevailing market prices, then re-rented to low income families at prices they can afford— with a subsidy to cover the difference. Subsidies have even been granted directly to individual low-income families to permit them to acquire housing "on their own."

In general, these pilot experiments appear to have worked out very well. Provisions in the Housing Act of 1965 will now permit subsidies to play a far more dynamic role in opening housing opportunities for minority families outside traditional areas of concentration. But their operation toward the objective of desegregation cannot be left to chance; it will require vigorous and imaginative guidance.

Another approach involving subsidies has been to grant indirect and limited subsidies to private non-profit sponsors through long-term mortgages financed directly from federal sources at interest rates below those available from private bankers. These mortgages encourage price levels low enough so that many families of modest income can qualify for new private housing.

In addition, several other forms of subsidy deserve investigation, particularly in regard to the occasional FHA- and VA-financed homes that become public property through foreclosure. The normal procedure is to put such homes up for sale through private brokers at an appraised "fair market value" and on an open-occupancy basis. The remarketing of these houses under reduced interest-rate mortgages, or even with direct subsidies, would provide additional stimulus to the dispersion of minorities.

93

5. *Comprehensive federal measures to increase the income of minorities.* Any measure which increases the purchasing power of racial minorities will bring a corresponding reduction in the economic obstacles to desegregation. Thus minimum wage floors should be raised, and federal resources should be directed toward expanding the number of jobs available, particularly for those of limited education. The work training programs created under anti-poverty and related legislation will help many minority group members qualify for better jobs, but qualifications will mean little if the jobs do not exist. Social service programs that aid individuals in making use of their full potential also help to a certain degree. But, basically, the need is for decent jobs at decent pay.

To be fully effective in countering segregation, moreover, social and economic measures must be linked far more closely than they are at present to patterns of residence. For example, minority members should be trained for the particular jobs that are opening up in the new commercial and industrial complexes now developing on the fringes of metropolitan areas. Simultaneous with this training, housing should be provided that enables residence reasonably close to such job opportunities. Incentives will have to be used to create the housing. Similarly, relocation from urban renewal areas should be coupled with a variety of services aimed at helping the displaced families to become more self-sufficient — particularly job-training and job-finding services. This criss-crossing of needs and techniques illuminates our first recommendation: that combating segregation demands comprehensive and coordinated planning. In this instance, if the activities are not coordinated the mismatch between available jobs and available people will continue—and housing will merely be a third disparate element in the conundrum.

6. *Intensified measures to improve the attractiveness of central cities.* Already under way through urban renewal and other programs are a number of efforts to lure more

affluent whites back to the cities. To a degree they have been successful—but not enough so as to halt the net loss of white population.

Physical improvement is vital, and it should be stepped up both through redevelopment and through rehabilitation, as well as through vigorous enforcement of housing codes. But probably more important to the goal is social renewal; and this is only now beginning on a substantial scale. Good schools are an essential attraction for middle-class families with children, white or Negro, yet the public schools are one of the weakest features of the major cities today. A few experimental schools in urban renewal areas have offered tangible evidence of what can be accomplished. But the need is for total renewal of entire school systems, not for mere token efforts.

Crime and violence are prime deterrents to middle-class residence in cities. The growing problem of crime in metropolitan areas frightens away the many whites who possess the economic flexibility to live where they choose. And it will continue to do so until the cities prove that they have the power to combat crime successfully. Still, the roots of crime lie so deep that achieving this end will be far from easy.

Poverty itself is far from attractive. It drives from its vicinity many of those who have been fortunate enough to escape its clutches themselves. The anti-poverty program now getting under way in many cities should be helpful in meeting this problem; but to solve it decisively will require many more billions than are currently being spent.

7. *Intensive enforcement of anti-discrimination measures; affirmative action to promote full compliance.* While we have indicated that anti-discrimination laws and measures cannot do the job alone, they are nonetheless a highly necessary item in the total complex of weapons against residential segregation. The coverage of existing legal measures should be extended; enforcement powers should be strengthened. Further, as many of the better law-enforce-

ment agencies in this field already recognize, their activities must be broadened to include not merely enforcement but also affirmative action to encourage full compliance with the spirit as well as the letter of the law.

In this respect, as in the others we have discussed, it is futile to provide mere legal guarantees of equal access to the housing supply as it now stands, without also overcoming the limitations of policy and practice that have made this supply essentially unequal for Americans of different race. Neither can reliance be placed upon the members of a minority conditioned by generations of disadvantage to carry the full burden of understanding and asserting their newly guaranteed rights. Affirmative measures must attack the subtler and more complex components of housing inequality and restricted residential patterns. These components include some federal practices which help to continue and extend segregation while superficially having no relationship to race; and those local laws and practices which condone or even encourage blockbusting, extortionate financing, and the myriad types of exploitation classed under the term "slumlordism." Minorities must be encouraged to take full advantage of their legal rights; nothing will do more to promote this than laws and law-enforcement agencies truly devoted to the equal opportunity of all citizens.

8. *Expanded support for "grass-roots" citizen effort.* As indicated earlier, individual private citizens banding together on a spontaneous "ad hoc" basis to promote equal housing opportunities have had impressive success in helping to change laws, practices, and attitudes across the nation. Where they have been able to obtain the backing of major civic, religious, and labor groups, their efforts have been far more effective than where they have had to work alone.

Most of the grass-roots efforts, however, have been meagerly financed and have had little coordination with other groups either locally or nationally. These factors have limited their effectiveness. What can be achieved through citizen initiative when even a limited amount of financial aid is available to enable paid staff to support and coordinate their efforts is indicated by experience in metropolitan Washington, where the American Friends Service Committee established a Metropolitan Washington Housing Program under a grant from the Eugene and Agnes E. Meyer Foundation. This program, in turn, was aided and informed by the National Housing Opportunities Program of the AFSC, which has well over a decade of fair-housing experience in major metropolitan areas of the North and West.

When the AFSC program started, fair-housing activity in Washington's suburbs was restricted to a single small group operating chiefly in Montgomery County, Maryland—probably one of the most "liberal" suburban areas in the nation, as well as one of the wealthiest. Within two years an active fair-housing committee was underway in the racially and socially conservative northern Virginia suburbs of Washington, where few of the most optimistic proponents of desegregation would have predicted that such an organization could come into being during the present decade.

But this example merely serves to illuminate the deficiency. What has been accomplished in suburban Washington through a limited amount of financial support could be achieved or perhaps excelled in many other areas with equivalent aid. While some of the more forward-looking national and local foundations have helped to keep a few fair-housing efforts alive, by and large foundation support for such activities has been meager and unreliable. Compared to the many millions spent annually by philanthropic organizations on other national problems of comparable or even lesser importance, the few thousands devoted to housing segregation have been infinitesimal. This, then, is still another way in which national resources must be redirected if the problem is to be solved.

9. *A national educational campaign to promote public*

97

awareness of the problem and help achieve consensus as to the effort needed to combat it. The efforts of civil rights proponents to bring to public consciousness the problems of segregation and discrimination have been strikingly successful in recent years. For the first time in their history the American people appear generally aware that discrimination and segregation are destructive of the goals of democracy. So drastically have attitudes changed that a recent national poll showed that a substantial majority of white Americans felt they would neither move away nor take any hostile action if a Negro family moved next door. While only a small minority said they would actively welcome members of another racial group, most of the rest seemed to view desegregation as inevitable — and racially hostile behavior as socially unacceptable.

But it is a long stride forward from a neutral or resigned attitude toward desegregation on the part of most of the white public to a vigorous and affirmative effort to remove residential segregation from its key position in American life. The mustering of national resources necessary to accomplish this end will require a type and degree of comprehension and commitment on the part of all the public, majority and minority alike, that is commensurate to the problem at hand. It is this above all that must be generated.

Within the framework of American democracy, national consensus is most readily and desirably achieved through full awareness of the problem at hand and stimulation of public debate as to the best means of solution. Therefore, a national campaign to bring the facts of the situation to the attention of the public by every means available is the first order of the day. If public understanding and support are to reach the necessary levels, this campaign must begin immediately, before residential segregation has achieved even larger proportions than at present. If the statistics of the 1960 census have helped to shock some Americans into an awareness of the dilemma they have created for themselves, those of 1970 may convince many that the problem is too large to be solved. Some tangible progress, or at least a plan of action, must be evident before that time—or else discouragement may rule.

The core of organized citizen support with which such a campaign may be mounted is already in existence. It includes the National Committee Against Discrimination in Housing, representing as it does the interests of dozens of civic, religious, and labor organizations at the national level. Of key importance also is the National Housing Opportunities Program of the American Friends Service Committee with its local action programs in a number of areas. The Anti-Defamation League of B'nai B'rith has supported the gathering and promulgation of factual knowledge on the problem. Added to these are the substantial resources of hundreds of citizen fair-housing organizations across the country. But their efforts must be coordinated, focused, and above all adequately financed. And they must be recognized in such related fields as urban planning.

This book attempts to present a challenge as well as a small contribution to the task of building public awareness of the facts of the problem. The task of following through rests, as always, with the American people as a whole—led, as in every major struggle in their history, by a small group of devoted citizens with the clarity of vision to see the goal, and with the courage and the persistence to keep that goal in view despite all obstacles.

If they do not succeed, the result will almost certainly be the continued spread of the Negro ghettos; large-scale physical blight stemming from pressures generated within the captive Negro market; economic loss to many citizens of both races; persistent social disorder; and spreading racial inequities and tensions which strike at the very foundations of a free and democratic society. The choice, then, is not merely between segregation and desegregation —but between wholesale destruction of property and human values and the continued growth and security of American society itself.

99

NOTES

I. THE TASK AT HAND

1. Unless otherwise indicated, these and all other statistics which deal with population and housing characteristics are drawn from the U.S. Censuses of Population and Housing, which can be found in any well-stocked public library. These censuses, taken at the beginning of every decade, are the nation's most valuable storehouse of data on many social and economic problems.

2. Municipal governments must now confront the problem of race in many of their decisions. For an overview of local governmental action vis-à-vis race as of the early 1960's accompanied by a good bibliography, see "The City Government and Minority Groups," *Management Information Service,* International City Managers Association, Report No. 229, Feburary 1963. This report may be obtained from the Potomac Institute of Washington, D.C., which participated in its preparation. See also many of the publications of the U.S. Commission on Civil Rights dealing with local practices in housing, employment, etc. But the extent to which racial considerations now affect local decisions in many subject areas is only scantily documented.

3. The problem of de *facto* educational segregation and the civic conflict it often creates has been widely discussed in public print.

NOTES

The *New York Times Index* is an especially useful source. For more scholarly treatments, see Max Wolff, ed., "Toward Integration of Northern Schools," *Journal of Educational Sociology*, February 1963. Also, "Public School Segregation and Integration in the North," *Journal of Intergroup Relations*, November 1963. A provocative view on the feasibility of desegregation will be found in James B. Conant, *Slums and Suburbs*, New York, 1961.

4. The impact of race upon urban renewal, and vice versa, has been touched upon in many places. Among them: Robert C. Weaver, "Class, Race and Urban Renewal," *Land Economics*, August 1960. Also L. K. Northwood, "The Threat and Potential of Urban Renewal," *Journal of Intergroup Relations*, Spring 1961; and H. W Reynolds, "The Human Element in Urban Renewal," *Public Welfare*, April 1961. For an optimistic view on the consequences of renewal for displaced families, see *The Housing of Relocated Families*, a summary of a Bureau of the Census survey of families recently displaced from urban renewal sites, published by the Housing and Home Finance Agency, Washington, D.C., in March 1965. The "pro-renewal" viewpoint is also presented in *New Patterns in Urban Housing*, Experience Report 104, published by the U.S. Conference of Mayors, Community Relations Service, Washington, D.C., May 15, 1965.

5. There is a vast literature on the implications for local government of the divergence between population patterns and political boundaries in today's metropolitan areas. For an overview of governmental efforts to cope with the resulting problems, see Roscoe C. Martin, *Metropolis in Transition: Local Government Adaptation to Changing Urban Needs*, Washington, Housing and Home Finance Agency, September 1963. This study contains an extensive bibliography. An early and prescient discussion of the racial implications of metropolitan population shifts will be found in Morton Grodzins, *The Metropolitan Area as a Racial Problem*, Pittsburgh, 1958. While Grodzins' prescriptions for solution sometimes seem a bit naive in retrospect, his dramatic presentation of the problem has been amply confirmed by later knowledge. A provocative discussion of the suburbanites' viewpoint toward metropolitan area-wide cooperation toward solution of urban problems will be found in Charles R. Adrian, "Metropology: Folklore and Field Research," *Public Administration Review*, Summer 1961.

6. For a discussion of the implications of rapid land consumption for metropolitan Philadelphia, see George W. Grier, *Penjerdel: Region in Transition*, Philadelphia, Penjerdel, Inc., 1964.

7. An enlightening insight into the extent of recent urban expansion can be gained from a perusal of the 1960 *U.S. Census of Population*, especially the *U.S. Summaries*. The map which shows the boundaries of the 212 Standard Metropolitan Statistical Areas is especially striking. The most intensive treatment of the topic, as it affects the heavily urbanized northeastern seaboard of the U.S., will be found in Jean Gottman, *Megalopolis*, New York, 1961.

8. *A Plan for the Year 2000—The Nation's Capital*, prepared by the

National Capital Regional Planning Council, Washington, D.C., 1961. Some other major cities have also developed, or are in the process of developing, "Year 2000 Plans."

9. The relationship of racial factors to the Washington metropolitan plan is discussed in George B. Nesbitt and Marian P. Yankauer, "The Potential for Equal Housing Opportunity in the Nation's Capital," *Journal of Intergroup Relations,* Winter 1962-1963.

10. George Schermer, "Desegregation: A Community Design," *ADA News,* published by the Philadelphia Chapter of Americans for Democratic Action, July 1960. (Statistics somewhat revised by the author in light of subsequent information.)

11. Older central neighborhoods which once were well on the way to complete desertion by whites, but now are experiencing a reverse migration by whites of high socio-economic status, are now to be found in many cities. In Washington they include the Capitol Hill and "Neighbors, Inc." areas; in Philadelphia, Powelton Village and the near-central sections of Spruce and Pine Streets.

II. THE SPREAD OF SEGREGATION

1. For a detailed discussion of recent population shifts and their bearing on racial patterns of residence, see George and Eunice Grier, "Obstacles to Desegregation in America's Urban Areas," *Race,* July 1964. Dramatic maps showing the growth of Negro ghettos in Chicago will be found in Charles E. Silberman, "The City and the Negro," *Fortune,* March 1962. The topic has received intensive treatment by local scholars in a number of major cities. See, for example: Mildred Zander and Harold Goldblatt, *Trends in the Concentration and Dispersion of White and Non-White Residents of New York City, 1950-1960,* New York City Commission on Human Rights, Research Report No. 14. Also: Donald J. Bogue and D. P. Dandekar, *Population Trends and Prospects for the Chicago-Northwestern Indiana Consolidated Metropolitan Area: 1960 to 1990,* Chicago Population Research and Training Center, March 1962. Also: Martha Lavell, *Philadelphia's Non-white Population, 1960. Report No. 1: Demographic Data,* Philadelphia Commission on Human Relations, November 1961. Readers interested in similar analyses for their own areas may find that useful studies have been done by their municipal human relations agency or by the sociology department of a local university.

2. The phenomenon of rapid Negro population growth in the medium-sized cities is discussed in Eunice and George Grier, "The Negro Migration," *Housing Yearbook,* published by the National Housing Conference, Washington, D.C., 1960 and 1962. Also in another paper by the same authors: *The Impact of Race on Neighborhood in the Metropolitan Setting,* Washington, D.C., Washington Center for Metropolitan Studies, 1961.

3. The best discussions of the origin and development of segregated patterns of residence are still to be found in Robert C. Weaver, *The Negro Ghetto,* New York, 1948; and in Charles Abrams, *For-*

bidden Neighbors, New York, 1955. Both books, though relatively old, are in no sense outdated. They deserve reading by all interested in the problem.

4. For analyses and projections of metropolitan growth see Jerome P. Pickard, *Metropolitanization of the United States*, Research Monograph No. 2, Urban Land Institute, Washington, D.C., 1959. Also see "U.S.A. Population Changes 1950-1960," *Population Bulletin*, published by the Population Reference Bureau, Inc., Washington, D.C., March 1960. Again, while dealing with only a portion of the U.S., Gottman's *Megalopolis* is an invaluable source. A general discussion of metropolitan growth, set in historical perspective, will be found in "The Metropolitan Area Explosion: The Facts," Chapter Four of Philip M. Hauser, *Population Perspectives*, New Brunswick, N.J., 1960. This topic has been treated in many other places as well, and a complete bibliography would require many pages.

5. The indirect racial effects of federal housing policies are discussed in Bertram Weissbourd, *Segregation, Subsidies and Megalopolis*, Santa Barbara, Calif., Center for the Study of Democratic Institutions, 1964; also, in more detail, in an unpublished paper by Eunice and George Grier, "Federal Powers in Housing Affecting Race Relations," prepared for the Potomac Institute and the Washington Center for Metropolitan Studies in September 1962 (available on loan from the authors upon request).

6. *Our Non-white Population and Its Housing: The Changes Between 1950 and 1960*, Washington, D.C., Housing and Home Finance Agency, July 1963.

7. The history of opposition to public housing by the white residents of many suburbs—and for that matter, by the predominantly white populations of some central cities—is a long one, well documented in the press. One of the more thorough explorations of the reasons behind this opposition will be found in Donald H. Bouma, *Why Kalamazoo Voted No: The Defeat of a Housing Proposal*, Upjohn Institute for Employment Research, June 1962.

8. Chester Rapkin and William G. Grigsby, *The Demand for Housing in Eastwick*, prepared under contract for the Redevelopment Agency of the City of Philadelphia by the Institute for Urban Studies, University of Pennsylvania, Philadelphia, 1960.

9. See *Housing*, Book Four of the *1961 Report of the Commission on Civil Rights*, Washington, D.C.

10. The federal role in enforcing housing discrimination is documented in Abrams, *Forbidden Neighbors*, and in Eunice and George Grier, *Privately Developed Interracial Housing*, Berkeley, 1960. The latter volume contains, in Chapter Eight, detailed case histories of two post-World War II developments intended for interracial occupancy which were driven to financial ruin by FHA opposition, despite powerful private support.

11. Abrams, in *Forbidden Neighbors*, documents in some detail the form and use of racial and religious restrictive covenants. Their use against Jews in particular is explored in N. C. Belth, ed., *Barriers:*

Patterns of Discrimination Against Jews, New York, Anti-Defamation League, 1958.

12. See Benjamin R. Epstein and Arnold Forster, *Some of My Best Friends . . . ,* New York, 1962.

13. See George and Eunice Grier, "Obstacles to Desegregation in America's Urban Areas."

14. A particularly valuable discussion of the factors contributing to the Negro migration to urban areas, together with an assessment of its meaning for Negroes' political and economic status, can be found in Robert C. Weaver, "Urbanization of the Negro," a chapter in his *The Urban Complex,* New York, 1964.

15. Eunice S. Grier, *Understanding Washington's Changing Population,* Washington, D.C., Washington Center for Metropolitan Studies, 1961.

16. From Eunice S. Grier, *Understanding Washington's Changing Population.*

17. See *A Proposed Anti-Discrimination Housing Ordinance for the District of Columbia,* Summary of Hearing, Staff Statistical Investigation, and Finding of the Board of Commissioners, Washington, D.C., Government of the District of Columbia, March 1963.

18. Lavell, *Philadelphia's Non-white Population, 1960. Report No. 1: Demographic Data.*

19. Zander and Goldblatt, *Trends in the Concentration and Dispersal of White and Non-white Residents of New York City, 1950-1960.*

III. THE COSTS OF SEGREGATION

1. There have been many studies of the relationship of race to housing quality in local areas. Among the more recent are Harold Goldblatt, *The Cost and Quality of Housing in White and Negro Areas of New York City, 1960,* Research Report No. 7, New York City Commission on Human Rights, 1961; Martha Lavell, *Philadelphia's Non-white Population, 1960, Report No. 2: Housing Data,* Commission on Human Relations, City of Philadelphia, May 1962; Sara Hartman, *Rent and Housing Conditions by Race, Baltimore, Maryland, 1960,* Baltimore Urban Renewal and Housing Agency, September 1963; Barbara W. Scott, *The Status of Housing of Negroes in Pittsburgh,* Commission on Human Relations, City of Pittsburgh, May 1962.

2. This study is probably the best statistical analysis of the relationship between race and housing quality ever published. It has been digested as part of John B. Duncan and Albert Mindlin, "Municipal Fair Housing Legislation: Community Beliefs and Facts," *Phylon,* Fall 1964. In considerably more detail, with excellent tables and charts, the same study appears as part of a report of the District of Columbia government: *A Proposed Anti-Discrimination Housing Ordinance for the District of Columbia,* Washington, D.C., March 1963.

NOTES

3. Luigi Laurenti, *Property Values and Race,* Berkeley, 1960. Laurenti analyzes in depth data specially gathered in Philadelphia, San Francisco, and Oakland, California, during the mid-1950's. He also summarizes the work of other investigators in Chicago, Kansas City, Detroit, and Portland, Oregon. One of the Chicago studies examined was made in 1930. Despite the difference in time and conditions, its conclusions differed surprisingly little from those of other investigations performed a generation later. Since the Laurenti work appeared, additional studies of the property values question have been made in other communities. One of the more notable and recent is Erdman Palmore and John Howe, "Residential Integration and Property Values," *Social Problems,* Summer 1962. While there is a common tendency to believe that one's own community must be unique in its attitudes and behavior with regard to racial matters, the various studies are striking in the similarity of their findings.

4. Probably the most thorough and telling analysis of the economics involved in racial turnover mediated by real estate speculators was published by the Chicago Commission on Human Relations, a municipal agency, in 1962. In a single block which had changed from all-white to virtually all-Negro, with heavy involvement by speculators, the differential between the price paid by the speculator and that paid by the Negro buyer upon purchase under an installment contract ranged from 35 to 115 percent, with an average of 73 percent. The installment contract itself is a financing device which yields higher than average returns to the entrepreneur, so the profiteering only began with the sale. In Philadelphia, Rapkin and Grigsby found that absentee speculators in a racially changing area more than doubled their investments, on the average, within less than two years. Profits on sales to the first Negro buyer in an area were even higher; thus, the Negro family that "breaks the block" usually pays even more heavily than those who follow. See Chester Rapkin and William Grigsby, *The Demand for Housing in Racially Mixed Areas,* Berkeley, 1960.

5. *A Proposed Anti-Discrimination Housing Ordinance for the District of Columbia.*

6. *Mortgage Availability for Non-whites in the Chicago Area: A Report,* City of Chicago, Commission on Human Relations, April 1963.

7. The pain caused to long-time residents of ethnic neighborhoods by forced relocation in connection with urban renewal has been documented in Marc Fried, "Grieving for a Lost Home," in Leonard J. Duhl, ed., *The Urban Condition,* New York, 1963. No doubt much the same kind of agony is caused when long-established white residents are "forced" to give up their homes in changing neighborhoods through the activities of blockbusters.

8. For one exploration of the reactions of white residents to Negro entry see Eleanor P. Wolf, "Racial Transition in a Middle-Class Area," *Journal of Intergroup Relations,* Summer 1960. For another, see Eleanor Leacock, Martin Deutsch, and Joshua A. Fishman, *Toward*

Integration in Suburban Housing: The Bridgeview Study, New York, Anti-Defamation League, 1965.

9. For two explanations of the Levittown episode, see Marvin Bressler, "The Myers Case: An Instance of Successful Racial Invasion," *Social Problems*, Fall 1960; and Eunice and George Grier, "The Levittown Incident in Perspective," *Journal of Intergroup Relations*, July 1958.

10. See note 1, Chapter One, for references on local governmental action *vis-à-vis* race.

11. See note 2, Chapter One, for references on the problem of "de facto" educational segregation.

12. The impact of population dynamics on the schools of Washington is explored in Eunice S. Grier, *Understanding Washington's Changing Population*, and in George W. Grier, *The Changing Age Profile: Implications for Policy Planning in Metropolitan Washington*, Washington, D.C., Washington Center for Metropolitan Studies, 1964.

IV. THE UPSURGE OF CIVIC CONCERN: GOVERNMENTAL POLICY

1. See Abrams, *Forbidden Neighbors*, and Epstein and Forster, *Some of My Best Friends* . . .

2. One of the best sources of information on the activities of local fair-housing groups is *Trends in Housing*, published bi-monthly by the National Committee Against Discrimination in Housing, 323 Lexington Avenue, New York 10016.

3. The most complete and reliable source of up-to-date information on the status of housing anti-discrimination laws and ordinances throughout the nation is *Trends in Housing* (see note 2 above). A comprehensive analysis of action at all governmental levels up to the period just before the Federal Executive Order of 1962 will be found in Margaret Fisher and Frances Levenson, *Federal, State and Local Action Affecting Race and Housing*, National Association of Intergroup Relations Officials, September 1962. The texts of state and local laws as of the end of 1961 are summarized in *State Statutes and Local Ordinances Prohibiting Discrimination in Housing and Urban Renewal Operations*, published by the Housing and Home Finance Agency, Washington, D.C., December 1961.

4. A more detailed analysis of this question appears in an unpublished paper by the authors, "Federal Powers in Housing Affecting Race Relations," prepared for the Potomac Institute and the Washington Center for Metropolitan Studies, September 1962.

5. A discussion of racial restrictive covenants, their form and their application, will be found in Abrams, *Forbidden Neighbors*.

6. Case histories of two developments forced out of business by federal opposition to their open racial policies appear in Eunice and George Grier, *Privately Developed Interracial Housing*.

7. Patterns like this, once established, are not easily changed.

Even today, segregated public housing projects can be found in many localities where local or state ordinances prohibit discrimination. See *Trends Toward Open Occupancy in Low-Rent Housing Programs of the Public Housing Administration*, published at intervals by the Public Housing Administration, Washington, D.C.

8. Charles Abrams, "The Housing Order and Its Limits," *Commentary*, January 1963.

9. Gunnar Myrdal, *An American Dilemma*, New York, 1944.

10. An examination of the early consequences of the decision, including initial efforts to thwart it, will be found in B. T. McGraw and George B. Nesbitt, "Aftermath of Shelley vs. Kraemer on Residential Restriction by Race," *Land Economics*, August 1953. Three years later, Nesbitt reviewed the same question in "Dispersion of Non-white Residence in Washington, D.C.: Some of its Implications," *Land Economics*, August 1956. A further re-examination of the effects of the decision, a decade after the first, will be found in Nesbitt and Yankauer, "The Potential for Equal Housing Opportunity in the Nation's Capital."

11. The group referred to is Friends Suburban Housing, Inc., with offices in Ardmore, Pennsylvania.

12. See Edward Rutledge and William R. Valentine, "Cooperation Agreements in Housing Administration," *Journal of Intergroup Relations*, Summer 1960.

13. *Trends Toward Open Occupancy in Low Rent Housing Programs of the Public Housing Administration*.

14. Abrams, "The Housing Order and its Limits." For another discussion of some of the limitations of the order, as well as a legal rationale for its extension, see Martin E. Sloane and Monroe H. Freedman, "The Executive Order on Housing: The Constitutional Basis for What it Fails to Do," *Howard Law Journal*, Winter 1963.

15. See *Trends in Housing*, published by the National Committee Against Discrimination in Housing; and *Federal, State and Local Action Affecting Race and Housing*, prepared by the National Association of Intergroup Relations Officials and also available from NCDH.

16. For a discussion of this problem, see Northwood, "The Threat and Potential of Urban Renewal." Also H. W. Reynolds, "What Do We Know About Our Experiences with Relocation?", *Journal of Intergroup Relations*, Autumn 1961.

V. THE UPSURGE OF CIVIC CONCERN: PRIVATE CITIZEN ACTION

1. A nationwide study that examined the experiences of some fifty private housing developments open from the outset to interracial occupancy is reported in Eunice and George Grier, *Privately Developed Interracial Housing*. A more recent but less comprehensive compilation of experience, which leads nonetheless to many of the same conclusions, is found in *Equal Opportunity in Housing—*

A *Series of Case Studies,* Washington, D.C., Housing and Home Finance Agency, June 1964.

2. The experiences of various neighborhoods with efforts to achieve racial stabilization have been discussed in the public prints, oftentimes in local newspapers. Among the more valuable studies on this topic are: Julia Abrahamson, *A Neighborhood Finds Itself,* New York, 1949; and Leacock, Deutsch and Fishman, *Toward Integration in Suburban Housing: The Bridgeview Study.* The first of these, about the Hyde Park-Kenwood Community Conference in Chicago at an early stage in its existence, is highly optimistic. The second, about a neighborhood stabilization effort in a suburban area of a large eastern metropolis, encompasses almost a decade of experience. The picture it presents is considerably less bright but more objective and probably more representative.

3. An excellent presentation of techniques which have been found useful in efforts to promote open-housing opportunities in neighborhoods formerly closed to Negroes is contained in Margaret Fisher and Charlotte Meacham, *Fair Housing Handbook,* published jointly by the National Committee Against Discrimination in Housing and the American Friends Service Committee, 1964. See also various issues of *Trends in Housing.*

4. Syracuse Friends Housing Committee, "Report of a Housing Project," Syracuse, 1955.

5. *Equal Opportunity in Housing—Challenge to American Communities,* New York, National Committee Against Discrimination in Housing, 1963.

6. Clarence Hunter, "Barriers Fall—105 Negro Homes in All-White Areas," *The Evening Star,* Washington, D. C., January 7, 1965. Similar news stories about the efforts of fair-housing groups in other major metropolitan areas may be obtained in reprint form from the National Committee Against Discrimination in Housing and the American Friends Service Committee.

INDEX

DATE DUE			
FEB 22 71			
APR 29			
DEC 3 '74			
DEC 9 74			
DEC 18 '75			
DEC 1 82			

GAYLORD M-2

PRINTED IN U.S.A.